Luther M. Maddy, Ph.D.

Well done!

Ten keys to remaining faithful to the end

Idaho, USA

Well done: Ten keys to remaining faithful to the end

All Scripture quotations, unless otherwise indicated, are taken from the Holy Bible, New International Version®, NIV®. Copyright ©1973, 1978, 1984, 2011 by Biblica, Inc.™ Used by permission of Zondervan. All rights reserved worldwide. www.zondervan.com The "NIV" and "New International Version" are trademarks registered in the United States Patent and Trademark Office by Biblica, Inc.™

Copyright © 2019 Luther M. Maddy III
Paperback ISBN: 978-0-578-48231-6

All rights reserved. No part of this book may be reproduced or transmitted in any form other by any means, electronic or mechanical, including photocopying and recording or by any information storage and retrieval system, without permission in writing from the publisher.

Published by Finish Line Press, Idaho, USA

Acknowledgements

This book would not have been possible without the positive influence of many people in my life, most of whom are not highlighted in these pages. I wish to thank my mother, the pastors, youth workers, mentors, and Sunday school teachers who did not give up on me. Thank you for your influence and for diligently praying for me. Since many of these individuals have gone on to glory, I look forward to thanking them personally.

I wish also to thank my wife Tracy, who continually challenges me to strive to reach my potential.

The editing suggestions of Debbie Goodwin, Dr. Brett Morris, and Bret Baxter are greatly appreciated. Some of the names mentioned in these pages have been changed to avoid embarrassing those individuals.

Contents

Introduction 1
#1 Don't let your age define you 7
#2 Maintain an eternal focus 27
#3 Use your influence for the Kingdom 49
#4 Never stop learning and growing 69
#5 Don't give up before you're done 87
#6 Learn from your past mistakes.....................................103
#7 Take charge of your time, energy, and finances 127
#8 Learn from the Lord's discipline 141
#9 Don't fear the future 163
#10 Pursue an eternal crown 179

Introduction

When I began this book, I was very close to my 60th birthday. That is the main reason for my sitting down and beginning to write. This book is, first and foremost, my personal manifesto. It represents my ideal for myself: What I want to aspire to, not what I have already achieved.

I did not intend the "ten keys" included in this book to be taken as a blueprint or guaranteed path to Christian maturity. The "ten keys" simply represent things I have learned and continue to learn.

Neither did I intend this book to be a critique of others. However, if by reading what I intended as encouragement to myself, you are inspired and motivated to continue serving the Lord into your

Introduction

golden years and beyond, then my exhortations have exceeded my original intentions and I will be considerably blessed.

Society and even some churches may seem to marginalize people after they reach a certain age. In 1967, the United States made discrimination based on age illegal. The starting age for being protected is only 40. From where I stand now, that seems very young.

Yet, despite being often sidelined, we as middle agers, seniors, and the elderly represent a vast pool of wisdom and experience that is often untapped and ignored. Rather than being relegated to obscurity and trivialization, those of us in or approaching retirement have the potential to be members of a massive army of mature believers that can change the world, one person at a time.

It is my hope that after reading this book you will realize your own potential and will be inspired and motivated to use your gifts more fully for the Lord. I also hope and pray that believers in leadership, regardless of their age, will become more aware of the potential of those sitting in their pews who may simply be waiting for the encouragement to be unleashed for the Lord.

Every believer has value in the Kingdom and an important role within it. Your role may seem small to you, but as Paul explained in I Corinthians 12, every part of the Body is essential. Please realize that you remain valuable in His kingdom, regardless of your age or physical abilities. You still have work to do, but that may require some sacrifices as you carry your cross. But if you picked up this book, you probably realize this already.

We are not excused from His service because we start getting gray hair or retire. No, we should continue working at what He has called us to do until the day He calls us home. Regardless of our age, we need to continue serving right where we are and also look for additional opportunities as He presents them. The process of maturing in the knowledge and practice of our faith should never end. Our quest to become more like Christ should continue daily until we finally become like Him in fullness.

Introduction

It is my hope that this book encourages and prods you, if only just a little, to persevere, to finish the race well, to put your full effort in focusing on the things that matter for eternity, and to use the remaining portion of your life to build on the foundation laid by Christ with gold, silver, and precious stones. Should you leave this book somewhat convicted, then it has served its purpose. I am there with you. However, please don't leave these pages thinking you are so lacking and failing in His service that you give up completely in despair. Remember the old clichés about eating an elephant one bite at a time, or that Rome took more than a day to build. If you see areas where change is warranted, focus on something you can easily change or accomplish.

Charles Spurgeon provided excellent advice when he said, "The way to do a great deal is to keep on doing a little. The way to do nothing at all is to be continually resolving that you will do everything.[1]" Little by little, you and I both can become more like

Introduction

It is my hope that this book encourages and prods you, if only just a little, to persevere, to finish the race well, to put your full effort in focusing on the things that matter for eternity, and to use the remaining portion of your life to build on the foundation laid by Christ with gold, silver, and precious stones. Should you leave this book somewhat convicted, then it has served its purpose. I am there with you. However, please don't leave these pages thinking you are so lacking and failing in His service that you give up completely in despair. Remember the old clichés about eating an elephant one bite at a time, or that Rome took more than a day to build. If you see areas where change is warranted, focus on something you can easily change or accomplish.

Charles Spurgeon provided excellent advice when he said, "The way to do a great deal is to keep on doing a little. The way to do nothing at all is to be continually resolving that you will do everything.[1]" Little by little, you and I both can become more like

Well done: Ten keys to remaining faithful to the end

be waiting for the encouragement to be unleashed for the Lord.

Every believer has value in the Kingdom and an important role within it. Your role may seem small to you, but as Paul explained in I Corinthians 12, every part of the Body is essential. Please realize that you remain valuable in His kingdom, regardless of your age or physical abilities. You still have work to do, but that may require some sacrifices as you carry your cross. But if you picked up this book, you probably realize this already.

We are not excused from His service because we start getting gray hair or retire. No, we should continue working at what He has called us to do until the day He calls us home. Regardless of our age, we need to continue serving right where we are and also look for additional opportunities as He presents them. The process of maturing in the knowledge and practice of our faith should never end. Our quest to become more like Christ should continue daily until we finally become like Him in fullness.

Well done: Ten keys to remaining faithful to the end

Christ as we choose daily to pursue the eternal rather than the temporal.

    Let us resolve, once and for all, to pursue the things that matter for eternity, to serve the Lord as long as we are able, and to make our ultimate goal, not a life of leisure in our golden years, but an eternal crown. Let us diligently strive to begin eternity by laying that crown at the feet of Jesus, and hearing the words, "Well done, good and faithful servant."

With you in His service,

Luther (Monty) Maddy III, Ph.D.

#1
Don't let your age define you

No eye has seen, no ear has heard,
and no mind has conceived
what God has prepared for those who love him
I Cor 2:9

#2: Maintain an eternal focus

I am a Capricorn. This may seem a strange way to start a Christian book, so first let me assure you that I'm not a follower of astrology. If I haven't lost you already, let me provide some context for that statement.

Capricorns, or so I remember my fourth-grade teacher saying, are late bloomers. That is actually all I recall of my introduction to astrology in that public-school classroom. I assume the other students learned things about themselves as our teacher introduced us to our horoscopes and read the personality characteristics of each zodiac sign. These descriptions were probably generic enough to fit just about anyone.

While my teacher told me I would be a late bloomer, my ten-year-old mind had difficulty determining what that really meant. She did not define or clarify any of the personality traits we were supposedly stuck with, she just read them. Being a late bloomer could mean almost anything. Perhaps it meant I would be late leaving the fourth grade, late reaching puberty, late finding true love, late achieving career or financial success, late finding God's will for my life, or even late finding enjoyable hobbies to consume my leisure time. As you can see from this list, my definition of being a late bloomer changed as I grew older. That is the brilliance of any generic prophecy or personality description: Make it vague enough and it will perfectly explain any occasion or person.

    I grew up in church and knew even at that young age the biblical admonitions against astrology. Yet thinking I would be a late bloomer permeated every aspect of my life from that day forward. I have never been able to shake off that concept. While that may seem like a bad thing, thinking myself a late bloomer has come in handy on many occasions. I resorted to the late bloomer excuse, at least internally, whenever a business venture or job did not take off like I planned. Not earning my last college degree until I reached the age of fifty-four was no problem. I am just a late bloomer, so that meant I was right on track.

    Another advantage of being convinced I was a late bloomer was that it enabled me to recover from

#2: Maintain an eternal focus

failure rather quickly. No job. No money. No retirement savings. No problem. I just convinced myself that my best days were yet to come. I had not yet reached my peak. I would bloom eventually.

While it may seem surprising, the concept of being a late bloomer is actually quite biblical, at least when it comes to spiritual matters. We are told in Philippians 1:6 that God will complete what He started in us, even if it takes until we meet Jesus. And that is exactly how long it will take us to reach our spiritual peak. Only then will we truly bloom.

As I have matured in my faith and in age, I have come to realize that we are all late bloomers. We are all, or at least should be, on a journey to become more like Christ. Our quest for Christian maturity and Christ-likeness should never end. We should never reach a point where we say to ourselves, "I quit. I'm enough like Christ now. I don't need to go any further. I have served Christ all I need to. I have finally completed my spiritual journey. I have arrived."

While those statements sound silly, the concepts they represent often subtly creep into our thinking. As we mature in years, does attending and serving in our local church take second priority to our relaxation and enjoyment? Have we slowed down in our studying the Word and learning more of God? Have we decided we've bloomed enough? Instead, we should be diligently striving to reach full bloom as Christians, realizing that full bloom will not occur until Christ calls us home.

The Apostle Paul expressed this eloquently when he said:

> *I want to know Christ – yes, to know the power of his resurrection and participation in his sufferings, becoming like him in his death, and so, somehow, attaining to the resurrection from the dead. Not that I have already obtained this, or have already arrived at my goal, but I press on to take hold of that for which Christ Jesus took hold of me. Brothers and sisters, I do not consider myself yet to have taken hold of it. But one thing I do: Forgetting what is behind and straining toward what is ahead, I press on toward the goal*

#2: Maintain an eternal focus

> *to win the prize for which God has called me heavenward in Christ Jesus*[2].

When picturing examples of late bloomers, Paul probably does not immediately come to most people's minds. However, when Paul wrote this letter to the Philippians, he was neither a new believer nor a young man. In fact, he was very near the end of his ministry and his life. By the time he wrote this epistle to the Philippians, Paul had already started at least fourteen churches and had been on at least three harrowing missionary journeys. Yet, by his own admission, he had not yet reached his peak.

Even after all he had learned and experienced, Paul had not yet achieved his goal. He had still not bloomed as a fully mature Christian. Paul realized this would not happen until he met Christ, but that did not stop him from daily pursuing the goal of knowing Christ better and becoming more like Him.

While he certainly could have, Paul did not rest on his past accomplishments. He did not decide to take it easy in his later years, even when he was imprisoned. Tradition tells us that Paul was likely in or approaching his sixties when he wrote Philippians. Paul was mature in faith and age, but he approached everything he did with the attitude of knowing his best days were still in the future.

In the thirteenth chapter of Numbers we read about Caleb, an individual who kept his eye on the prize and did not stray from the path that led to achieving his goals. Caleb never deviated, even when his goal seemed impossible, even when it would have been easier to retire to the golf course. Instead, Caleb waited, trained, and matured for forty-five years until it was time to bloom to his fullest.

When we first meet Caleb, he is already forty years old. He was chosen to represent the tribe of Judah in the group of twelve spies or scouts Moses sent out to examine the land of Canaan that God promised the Israelites.

From what we know of him in scripture, it is safe to assume that Caleb was a man's man, a leader, and a man of influence. We don't know exactly how the twelve scouts were chosen, but most assuredly some

#2: Maintain an eternal focus

had already shown bravery and skill as warriors in the earlier battle against the Amalekites.

We know this was the case for Joshua. Before going into battle with the Amalekites, Moses selected Joshua to lead Israel's warriors to victory against that enemy. After he proved himself a capable leader, Moses also selected him as one of the twelve spies.

Moses sent the twelve scouts out to examine the land for forty days. Their assignment was to report their findings when they returned. The twelve returned with some of the produce – grapes - from the land they explored. All the scouts reported, some though with great reluctance, that the land did indeed flow with milk and honey. However, ten of the twelve scouts let fear rule them. They recounted being terrified by the land's current inhabitants, who were numerous, gigantic, powerful, and living in fortified cities.

Imagine the scene for just a moment when the tribal leaders gathered to hear the scouts report on their foray into the Promised Land. The negativity of the ten cowardly scouts struck fear into the hearts of the people. As they did quite often, the people began to complain. They even lamented they ever left their Egyptian slave masters. It was bad enough that Moses led them into the desert and gave them nothing to eat but manna and quail, but now he expected them to all be killed by giants as they crossed into the land God promised them.

The rebellious murmuring starts small, but soon the hushed voices grow louder until they reach near fever pitch. Anarchists are sneaking around trying to incite a revolution. Unless something happens quickly, the entire assembly will be calling for Moses to resign, or perhaps even be stoned.

Suddenly Caleb steps forward, his right hand firmly grasping the hilt of the sword in his belt. Then, with a booming voice, he silences the crowd and explains the true situation. "The land is ours for the taking. We can conquer everyone in it with ease. Don't you remember that God is on our side? Let's go now! On to battle!"

A hush falls over the crowd for a few minutes, but then the ten spineless scouts begin sniveling

#2: Maintain an eternal focus

again. "The people there are like giants and we're nothing but grasshoppers compared to them. We can't win in a fight against them. They will kill us all and rape our wives. They will take our children as slaves. Oh, the horror! Think of your children. We can't do this! Let's impeach Moses and get a leader who will take us back to Egypt!"

Mind you, it has been just over one year since these people left Egypt. They saw God curse Egypt with plagues, part the Red Sea, guide them day and night, and provide for their every need. Yet, they let their fear control them.

According to rabbinical literature, the ten fearful scouts were very reluctant to bring back fruit and other examples of the Promised Land's abundance. They were so frightened by the inhabitants they saw there that they did not want to bring back anything that might encourage the people to attempt to possess the land. Caleb strongly insisted they bring back some of the land's bounty, so much so that this tradition has him drawing his sword and saying, "If you will not take any fruit with you, then either my life or yours![3]"

Well done: Ten keys to remaining faithful to the end

    Caleb may have won the battle to return with fruits from the Promised Land, but the ten sniveling scouts won the people over this day. But it does not end well for them. Moses, with the Lord's help, regains control of the crowd. God, in His disappointment, relegates the people to forty years of wandering and sends a plague to wipe out all the spies except Caleb and Joshua.

    God singled out Caleb and acclaimed him for having a different spirit and following the Lord wholeheartedly. Because of Caleb's faithfulness, God promised that he would see and possess the Promised Land. Joshua and Caleb were the only members of the nation over the age of twenty-one to make it to the Promised Land. All the rest perished during the forty-year wilderness wandering God imposed because of the people's lack of faith. The Lord was ready to help them conquer and possess the land, but they were too fearful to act.

    Forty-five years pass before we run into Caleb again. In the fourteenth chapter of the book of Joshua, Caleb, now at the age of eighty-five, asks

#2: Maintain an eternal focus

something of Joshua, who took over command of the Israelites after Moses died. As leader of the people, Joshua is now in the process of dividing the land between Israel's twelve tribes.

Think about this carefully. If you were eighty-six and felt the president of your nation owed you a favor, what would you ask for? A comfortable home in Arizona? An ambassadorship to Switzerland or the Bahamas? A nice bonus to your retirement plan? A gold watch? While he could have requested a comfortable spot to sit in his rocking chair and watch the grass grow and sheep graze, Caleb wanted more. He wanted what God had promised to him. Caleb wanted to finally obtain his goal of possessing his tribe's portion of the Promised Land. Here is the conversation Caleb has with Joshua as recorded in scripture:

> *You know what the Lord said to Moses the man of God at Kadesh Barnea about you and me. I was forty years old when Moses the servant of the Lord sent me from Kadesh Barnea to explore the land. And I brought him back a report*

according to my convictions, but my fellow Israelites who went up with me made the hearts of the people melt in fear. I, however, followed the Lord my God wholeheartedly. So on that day Moses swore to me, 'The land on which your feet have walked will be your inheritance and that of your children forever, because you have followed the Lord my God wholeheartedly.

Now then, just as the Lord promised, he has kept me alive for forty-five years since the time he said this to Moses, while Israel moved about in the wilderness. So here I am today, eighty-five years old! I am still as strong today as the day Moses sent me out; I'm just as vigorous to go out to battle now as I was then. Now give me this hill country that the Lord promised me that day. You yourself heard then that the Anakites were there and their cities were large and fortified, but, the Lord helping me, I will drive them out just as he said.[4]

#2: Maintain an eternal focus

Caleb made it clear to Joshua that he was as fit as ever and still itching for the battle that should have occurred more than forty years earlier. He asked Joshua to assign to him and his family the land that God had promised. That was the land where the giant Anakites lived in their fortified cities. The Anakites lived in the hill country and had the built-in advantage of higher ground. But none of this dissuaded Caleb from pursuing his goal.

Caleb's best days did not begin until he was eighty-five. He implored the Lord's help and defeated his enemies and possessed the land he was promised. He did not give up in despair forty-five years earlier. No, he waited, albeit probably impatiently at times, maturing his faith and knowledge of God until his time came. He knew his best days were ahead of him during those forty years of wandering in the wilderness and he spent his time preparing and keeping his battle skills sharp. Scripture tells us that Caleb did indeed bloom. The Anakites were driven out and Caleb and his family possessed the land they were promised.

Well done: Ten keys to remaining faithful to the end

There are many other examples in Scripture of individuals who did not give up because they knew their best days were still ahead. One of those is the prophet Simeon, who Luke introduces to us in chapter two of his Gospel. Joseph and Mary arrived at the temple in Jerusalem when Jesus was just eight days old. As they reach the temple steps, they are quickly greeted by Simeon who was prompted by the Holy Spirit to show up at the temple that day.

God had previously told Simeon that he would not die until he had seen the Messiah. Realizing Jesus was the Messiah, Simeon felt he had fulfilled his purpose in life and was now ready to die. Luke does not tell us how old Simeon was, but we can assume he was not a young man.

It is also important to note that Simeon, though he was not at the temple when the call from God came, was ready and available. What if he had been out fishing on the Sea of Galilee on the day Jesus was presented at the temple? Or what if he had decided to spend the day at the camel races in Caesarea? Or what if he had decided to go camping for a week along

#2: Maintain an eternal focus

the Red Sea? You get the idea. Being used of God means being ready, always especially when you know you have a task ahead of you.

Luke does think it is important to discuss the age of another prophet, Anna. Luke tells us she was very old, at least eighty-four years old. Unlike Simeon, Anna did not just show up at the temple that special day, she apparently lived there. Luke tells us she was widowed after a seven-year marriage. Then, and after becoming widowed, she never left the temple area. She was there every day, worshipping, fasting, and praying, all the time knowing that her best days were still to come.

Other than recognizing Jesus as the Messiah when she saw him, we are not told that Anna received any special prompting from the Holy Spirit that day. Imagine then for just a moment, what it must have been like to be eighty-four in the time of Jesus. There was not a drug store on every corner where she could pick up a bottle of pain reliever. If she had arthritis, she just lived with the pain.

Well done: Ten keys to remaining faithful to the end

We will assume the Lord blessed Anna with good health, but at eighty-four, she was probably beginning to feel her age, if even just a little. Now, imagine if on the day Jesus arrived, Anna had decided to stay in bed just a little longer until the pain went away. She would have missed her entire calling. God could have prompted another prophet to show up and announce the Messiah, as He did with Simeon. But because Anna was faithfully worshipping at the temple every day for perhaps more than sixty years, she finally performed the task God had been preparing just for her.

It is important to note that none of the biblical characters mentioned here let themselves be limited by their age. They also refused to be defined by others when it came to their age. For instance, even in Joshua's time, eighty-five-year-old men did not lead armies into battle. This is probably why Caleb emphatically pointed out what great shape he was in. Had he listened to the naysayers around him, Caleb would have retired several years earlier and missed his destiny.

#2: Maintain an eternal focus

Think about Paul. Sixty-year old men shouldn't be running around the world on dangerous missionary journeys. If Paul had perhaps listened to those around him, he may have quit after two missionary journeys. Perhaps he would have only started ten churches. Perhaps he would have quit before writing some of the most important books in the New Testament.

Now back to Anna. Here she was an eighty-four-year-old woman standing in the courtyard of the temple every day, reminding all who would listen that the Savior of Israel was coming. It is possible that she had to endure criticism from some of the temple elders. Perhaps she was even asked to step down. Maybe they explained to her that people were tired of hearing from her and, quite frankly, looking at her. She was becoming bad for temple attendance. The money changers were suffering. It was time to promote a younger, more attractive prophet to greet people as they came to worship. If this was the case, Anna still stuck to what she knew to be right and persevered despite criticism.

Well done: Ten keys to remaining faithful to the end

What about you? Are you letting your age limit you? Are you letting others define what you can and cannot do?   Are you living in the past or preparing for the future? Do you look back on your past accomplishments with pride, or, like Paul, are you pressing on to the goal you haven't yet achieved? Are you training spiritually as an athlete trains? Are you patiently preparing for the time God will call you to do great things, like Caleb, Simenon, and Anna? To put it another way, are you content with a gold watch, or are you pursuing a golden crown?

Scripture shows us that God uses people who are willing to be used by Him. The people He uses are not quitters. They patiently endure, knowing their best days in God's service are still to come. God uses late bloomers, and that is what we should all be.

I firmly believe the concept of being a late bloomer should apply to every aspect of our lives, not just our relationship with Christ. We should face each day with the attitude that tomorrow we will bloom more than we did today. We should make every effort to find and stay on the path that leads us to become

#2: Maintain an eternal focus

more skilled in our profession, intellectually stimulated, better spouses, better parents, better grandparents, better friends, and above all better ambassadors for Christ. Every aspect of our multifaceted lives takes continual work. Becoming who we were truly designed by God to be does not happen automatically. Our goal should be to bloom in all areas of our life. Our best days are still ahead, and we will finally be completely fulfilled on the day we meet Christ.

God's plan to use us is not dependent on our age. He uses people of all ages. God's plan to use us is dependent on our willingness to be used. We might be only a benchwarmer for years, but if we continue training and preparing, our best days are still to come. We should strive to keep blooming a little every day until we reach full bloom on the day we meet Christ.

#2
Maintain an eternal focus

Only one life, 'twill soon be past
Only what's done for Christ will last
C.T. Studd

#2: Maintain an eternal focus

What are you living for? As Christians, we know our answer should be, "God, of course". But give that question some serious thought before you answer. What are you really living for? Your job? Your spouse? Your kids? Your grandkids? Your leisure activities? The ministries you are involved in?

Look at that list again. Is there an honest "yes" somewhere in the list? Probably. If so, does that mean you need to immediately fall to your knees and ask for forgiveness? Maybe. But, perhaps not.

There is nothing inherently wrong with enjoying the blessings God has given you. Those things and people that God blesses you with can bring joy and pleasure to your life. They can also bring grief, but that is for another chapter.

Enjoying our life here on earth is not inherently sinful. In discussing earthly wealth, Paul, in his letter to Timothy, tells us that "God richly provides us with everything for our enjoyment."[5] The problem arises when the foundation of our hope, security, and fulfillment becomes the people and things God has blessed us with.

It takes another set of questions to reveal the truth. What has first place in your heart? What do you value above all else? What are you basing your hope on? Is there some person or thing you don't think you could live without? What are you living for and, if needed, are willing to die for?

When asked which commandment was the greatest, Jesus responded you must "love the Lord your God with all your heart and with all your soul, and with all your mind.[6]" Loving God with all our heart, soul, and mind does not mean we have nothing left in us to love or enjoy others. On the contrary, loving God means you will love others with the Godly love that He provides. Loving God means you will still enjoy the people and things He has blessed you with. It also means, as you mature in your faith, those things and people will take their rightful place in your priority list after, the King of the Universe.

Three of the four gospels recount the story of the rich man who asked Jesus how he could receive

#2: Maintain an eternal focus

eternal life. Jesus responded by giving a synopsis of six of the Ten Commandments. The commandments Jesus summarized focused on the rich man's treatment of others: do not commit adultery, do not steal, do not murder, do not cheat, do not bear false witness, and honor your father and mother.

The commandments Jesus listed for the rich man pertained to the second greatest commandment, "Love your neighbor as yourself."[7] The rich man was quick to respond to Jesus by saying that he had not broken any of those commandments, even since he was a young boy. In other words, this rich man was devout and righteous on the outside, in the way he treated others. He was confident he had not broken the commandments that Jesus listed. As he recounted his obedience, he was probably sure he was well on his way to gaining eternal life, based on his own righteousness.

Despite this man's claim of being righteous, Jesus saw his heart and knew instantly what was truly important to him. Jesus knew this man held on to his wealth too tightly and did not have God as first place in his heart. This man lived for and based his security on his wealth. It was his wealth, not God, that he loved with all his heart, mind, and soul. Jesus saw beyond this man's self-righteous facade.

The rich man was not guilty of being rich. Instead, he was truly guilty of idolatry. He had placed another god - his wealth - above the true God. When Jesus told him to sell everything and give it away, this man was faced with a choice: trust and worship God or trust and worship his wealth. The story of this man ends with him walking sadly away.

The Bible does not tell us if this man later had a change of heart. Some have speculated he later repented and became a Christ follower. Some Bible teachers claim he was identified later in scripture as Barnabas, Joseph of Arimathea, Saul of Tarsus, or John Mark the author of the Gospel according to Mark.

All attempts to identify the rich man are nothing more than speculation, but Mark's gospel provides an interesting detail absent from Matthew and Luke. In Mark's version of this story, after the man confirms he

#2: Maintain an eternal focus

has followed all the commandments, Jesus looked at him and loved him.[8] Even though Jesus instantly knew this man he placed his wealth above God and thus was guilty of idolatry, Jesus still loved him. And the same is true for you and me. Hallelujah!

At some time in our lives, we are all guilty of idolatry. We have all placed someone or something ahead of God in our priority list. We have drawn comfort and security from something created, rather than from the Creator. But the good news is this does not lessen His love for us. He still loves us and waits for us to put Him in His rightful place as king of our lives.

One of the most difficult teachings of Jesus is found in the fourteenth chapter of Luke. In this passage Jesus instructs that his followers must hate their father, mother, wife, children, brothers, and sisters.[9] Jesus probably used the word hate in this lesson to get His hearers' attention. Once He had their attention, He went on to explain that following Him would be very costly. It could mean losing your family and even your own life. Esteeming any of these above

Well done: Ten keys to remaining faithful to the end

Him meant you were not ready to be His follower. Jesus is clearly teaching that to be one of His disciples, you must be willing to give up everything to pursue the most valuable relationship of all.

We don't often hear sermons about the cost of following Jesus. Think about what it cost Paul, Stephen, Peter, James, and millions more. Think about what it costs today to be a follower of Christ in some Muslim-dominated nations and in many places in Asia. Even in the United States, being a Christ follower can be very costly.

In a similar teaching recorded in the tenth chapter of Matthew, Jesus uses wording that is not as harsh. In this passage. Jesus explains that anyone who loves his family or own life more than he loves Jesus is not ready to be a Christ follower.[10] Even here, Jesus clearly explains that following Him will cost us everything.

The Apostle Paul understood this concept. He knew that placing anything above Christ would be disastrous. In the fourth chapter of Philippians, Paul makes this very clear when he said he considered

#2: Maintain an eternal focus

everything a loss compared to the greatness of knowing Christ. Paul continues to explain that everything he gave up was worthless garbage compared to gaining Christ.[11]

While your Bible translation may use the word garbage, or refuse, the original Greek word would probably be better translated as excrement, or manure. Some translations correctly use the word "dung" in this verse. Excrement or manure is exactly what Paul meant. On the day we stand before the Judgment Seat of Christ, anything in our lives that kept us from following Him fully will be nothing more than manure. That includes the blessings He has given us. Oh, that we could truly live understanding this fully!

Putting Christ in His rightful position as first in our hearts does not mean we must leave our families, take a vow of poverty, or live solitary lives in a monastery. Monasteries certainly have their purposes for some, but if all Christians cloistered themselves away from all unbelievers, we would have no influence on a world of people needing salvation. Instead, we are in the world but not of the world. We need to be shining Christ's light in the darkness: messengers of the good news of salvation and ambassadors of reconciliation. We need to develop an eternal perspective.

In His sermon on the Mount, Jesus clearly explained the concept of having an eternal perspective. In the sixth chapter of Matthew, Jesus discusses the futility of worrying about temporal things, including food, clothing, and even your lifespan. His message was simple. God is sovereign. He knows and cares about your needs. Instead of worrying, put your efforts into putting Him first. When you do this, all the other things will fall into place.[12]

In the tenth chapter of Mark, after the rich ruler walked away sadly, the disciples may have begun to feel a little prideful. Peter speaks up and reminds Jesus that he and the other disciples left everything to follow him. Peter was undoubtedly thinking about dropping his nets and walking away from his fishing business when Jesus called.

#2: Maintain an eternal focus

Jesus responded to Peter, not with rebuke, but with a commendation and a promise. All who have left people and things to follow Him, Jesus said, will be repaid in this life and the life to come. Jesus told the disciples that those who sacrificed for Him and the sake of the Gospel will receive a hundred times as many wives, children, families, and lands as they have given up to follow Him.

This is another time when Jesus was trying to get His hearers' attention with His choice of words. Jesus was not instituting the prosperity gospel that permeates our culture today, nor was he recommending polygamy. Clearly, the disciples did not become sultans in a castle, spending their time counting their wealth and their wives. This is not what Jesus meant. Instead, Jesus explained that what we receive from Him will be worth infinitely more than what we have given up for Him. What we give up when we put Christ in His rightful place is nothing more than dung compared to gaining Christ.

With an eternal, rather than temporal perspective, we will value things differently. Yes, we have been promised blessings. But those blessings may come only at our resurrection. Jesus is not promising a life of prosperity and ease. In fact, scripture is clear that in this life, we should expect suffering and difficulty. Knowing this should make us even more grateful for any blessings we do receive in this life.

In the "faith chapter", the eleventh chapter of Hebrews, the author lists heroes of the Old Testament as examples of those who lived by faith. The people listed in this chapter had an eternal perspective. After listing several famous and lesser-known Old Testament characters, the chapter concludes with "yet none of them received what had been promised."[13]

What had God promised that they did not receive? The Savior who came in the person of Jesus Christ. It did not end well for many mentioned in this chapter, Hebrews 11. Some were tortured, put in prison, stoned, or sawed in two. Some did great things and were blessed with great kingdoms and wealth. Yet, all in this list were commended, because they lived understanding the eternal was more valuable

#2: Maintain an eternal focus

than the temporal. They were willing to give up all for the sake of doing God's will, and they had faith in His promised redemption.

In the midst of writing this chapter, I began feeling quite proud of myself. I began mulling over the ministries in which I am involved with to build the Kingdom. I convinced myself I have given up much to follow Jesus, which even includes living in a small town several hours away from everyone in my family, except for my wife, Tracy.

Tuesday night of this week, we started a new semester of classes at a fledgling Bible college I founded with the encouragement of my pastor. I am not teaching this semester, but coordinating the four teachers, classrooms, and students was quite a task for our opening evening. After classes started, I stayed to provide moral support to my wife as she taught her class in apologetics. We finally made it home a little after nine that evening, after a long day of work and ministry. The next day I headed off for a two-day trip for my job that pays the bills.

Well done: Ten keys to remaining faithful to the end

Saturday morning of this week, which my wife and I often reserve as "our time" was spent at church. We attended a training for ministry leaders. The training lasted until noon. After a short, but relaxing, lunch out, my wife secluded herself in her study to prepare for the adult education class she was teaching at our church the next morning. Tracy earns her living as a registered nurse, but her love is teaching, which is why she pursued and earned a master's degree in theology.

The next morning found me preparing a Bible lesson for the home group that meets in our house every Sunday evening. Tracy was putting the last minute touches on that morning's lesson. As I found a stopping point in my lesson preparation, I once again began mulling over how much I was giving to the Lord. I was sure I deserved a "well done thou good and faithful servant", or at least a pat on the back.

As I was welling up with pride, I received a text from a man 10 years my junior, whom I occasionally advise and mentor. Mostly, I just listen. His text told me he needed to talk and wondered if I could spare

#2: Maintain an eternal focus

some time after church ended. Grudgingly, because that cut into our short period of relaxation between church and cleaning the house for home group, I agreed.

I trudged upstairs and announced to Tracy that our lunch plans would be delayed while I spent some time with this man. It was then she let me know that a young couple in our home group who lived several miles away asked to "hang out" at our house that afternoon. Tracy had told them the door would be unlocked, so I knew this meant they would already be there when we arrived home from lunch. Any plans I had for rest and relaxation Sunday afternoon were now history. Tracy, obviously sensing my bad attitude, mentioned that it appeared we would be in ministry all day long.

Later that Sunday, after Tracy completed her lesson, we attended worship service. After listening to the sermon, I listened to my friend. After that we were finally able to enjoy sitting down to a meal together in a restaurant. We rarely cook at home. There just is not enough time. My bad attitude though was getting worse. I was actually dreading going home because I would not be able to relax. I would have to be "on" for the couple hanging out at our house.

The unrighteous pride I felt earlier that day turned to frustration, perhaps even anger. I could not understand why God was demanding so much of me. I have given Him so much already. I was tired and just wanted a little time to relax.

As I was finishing up the last few French fries on my plate, my anger suddenly turned to understanding and then to guilt. Like the rich man who walked away sadly, I too was guilty of idolatry. I was valuing my time above the Lord. What was He asking of me? The answer was quite simple, He was asking for nothing less than everything.

Please don't think I am advocating that we minister until we drop dead from exhaustion. Certainly not. But God has an interesting way of making His children aware of the things they have placed above Him in their priority list. He sees right into our hearts and what we cherish the most is what He asks us to surrender to follow Him fully. For the

#2: Maintain an eternal focus

rich ruler, it was the security that comes from wealth. For me, at least this day, it was time.

After pleading for forgiveness under my breath, I mentioned my epiphany to Tracy. I even mentioned I was writing a chapter in this book dealing with this very thing. She responded that God certainly works that way. She mentioned she had learned long ago that her time was not her own. I believe her because I knew she would be spending her next two days preparing lessons.

The well-known couplet at the beginning of this chapter was penned by Charles Thomas Studd. Like the Apostle Paul, Studd was consumed with serving and knowing more of Christ. Born into a wealthy family in England in 1860, Studd achieved recognition for his cricket playing ability as a college student. He received Christ while he was still in college and that eventually set him on a completely different path.

A few years after his conversion, Studd decided to forego fame and fortune and become a missionary. When his wealthy father passed away, Studd donated almost all of his inheritance to ministries, including

Well done: Ten keys to remaining faithful to the end

Moody Bible Institute and the Salvation Army in India. When asked why he chose this direction for his life, his response was, "I know that cricket would not last, and honour would not last, and nothing in this world would last, but it was worthwhile living for the world to come."[14]

Charles T. Studd felt an unquenchable desire to win the lost for Christ. He served as a missionary in China, India, and Africa. He was instrumental in creating awareness for missions in both England and the United States. He founded a missionary organization known today as WEC (Worldwide Evangelism Crusade) International.

So driven by the desire to fully serve Christ, Charles became somewhat dismayed at the seeming lack of passion in so many Christians. Studd authored several books and pamphlets, most of which were designed to spur others to assist in the Great Commission. One of his most controversial works was titled "The D.C.D.". This title was from the assertion that true Christ followers "don't care a damn" about

#2: Maintain an eternal focus

anything that did not further the Kingdom of God. In that small booklet published in 1928, Studd wrote:

> *Oh, let us not rust out—let us not glide through the world and then slip quietly out.... At the very least let us see to it that the devil holds a thanksgiving service in hell, when he gets the news of our departure from the field of battle, and not merely spit in contempt.*
>
> *Let us blaze up and burn out, both ends and in the middle. Let us explode for Jesus and humanity.*
>
> *Paul...pretty well blew up every place he went to; let us follow him—and when we come to our last hour let us look at Samson and imitate his exit from the world; for confessing himself to be a failure, he prayed for strength to fight one more fight for his God and his people, and his prayer was heard.*

Well done: Ten keys to remaining faithful to the end

> *Let every good Christian be a D.C.D., and let every D.C.D. look at Samson and thus pray, "May my last end be like his," and indeed your prayer shall be answered....In Christ's glorious service let us reckon our own lives as of no account, and let us do so at once and be ready for everything...*

Studd used strong language to make his point, much like the Apostle Paul when he stated everything but Christ was excrement. Studd finished his work on earth at the age of 70, not in a retirement home or camping by the sea, but still working on the mission field in Africa. The ailment that finally brought about his demise was a bad gall bladder. He knew he was ill, but chose to forego treatment. Perhaps he just did not have the time to leave the mission field for treatment or surgery.

As Christians, we need to evaluate our lives daily. Are we living for manure or for the King of the Universe? Are we willing to ask God to help us "blaze up and burn out, both ends and in the middle"? Are we truly willing to "explode for Jesus and humanity"?

#2: Maintain an eternal focus

Are we living so that our last days will be like the Apostle Paul, C.T. Studd, or so many others that have paved the way for us? Or are we looking forward to a "much-deserved rest" at our summer home?

The choice is set before us daily. Whom or what will we serve? Rest assured, if you are not putting the Lord your God in His rightful place, the Holy Spirit will surely get to the heart of the matter.

Asking God to show us the idols in our lives is probably more dangerous than praying for patience. When He points out an idol in your life, He will ask you to remove it. Clearing out the idols may be as simple as rearranging your schedule, but it could be considerably more challenging. Ridding your life of those things, people, or attitudes that hinder your relationship with and service for Him may be quite painful. If you don't willingly loosen your grip, He may choose to rip them from you to get your attention.

Please don't leave this chapter thinking you need to sell everything you have, give up all your personal time, or move five hours or more from your family. If you sincerely ask, the Holy Spirit will bring to mind

Well done: Ten keys to remaining faithful to the end

those things that may be stumbling blocks in your relationship with Christ. If you, like me, are often guilty of idolatry, don't despair because, as He did with the rich ruler, Christ will look on us with love as He points out the things that need to change. When He does this, ask for forgiveness and, like Paul, press onward to the goal of perfection in Christ on the day that He returns. Until that day comes, enjoy the blessings He provides, but always remember everything is excrement compared to Christ.

#3

Use your influence for the Kingdom

The kingdom of heaven is like a mustard seed, which a man took and planted in his field. Though it is the smallest of all seeds, yet when it grows, it is the largest of garden plants and becomes a tree, so that the birds come and perch in its branches.
Matthew 13: 31-32

#3: Use your influence for the Kingdom

I am the product of a mixed marriage: a believing mother and an unbelieving father. My upbringing is certainly not unique. The New Testament tells us that Timothy had a believing mother and, from all indications, an unbelieving father. Like Timothy, my mother taught me much in the spiritual realm and ensured I attended church as a child.

While I certainly can't speak for Timothy, having an unbelieving father left an important void in my life: an example of Christian manhood. My paternal grandfather made no profession of faith until shortly before his death. My maternal grandfather professed Christ, but passed away before I was born. Only one of my several uncles professed Christ. From my early teens and into early adulthood I longed for something I had never actually observed, a model of Christian manhood in the home, in the workplace, in any aspect of life outside Sunday morning and evening church services.

As a young believer, I yearned to be mentored and discipled by an older Christian man. Someone who had faced the torrents of adolescence, early adulthood, and perhaps even a teenage marriage, yet remained true to his Christian faith. I loved and admired my father, but longed to share on a deeper level, which was not possible with an unbeliever. I prayed often for a friend, mentor, and male role model, but the Lord saw fit to leave those prayers unanswered until much later in my life. I have also consistently prayed for my father's salvation since I was old enough to realize the void in his life.

There were men in the church I attended as a child and teenager, but it seemed I was invisible to almost all of them. Most of the interactions I had with the men in the congregation, and even an occasional male Sunday school teacher, had minimal influence on me.

Fortunately, to one man at church I was not invisible and that resulted in his having a major impact on my life. Tony Storment's actions were small but profound and they affected me deeply. Tony sought me out every Sunday to shake my hand and tell me he was glad to see me at church. This started

#3: Use your influence for the Kingdom

when I was five and continued until I left home to join the military at the age of 18.

Tony's simple act of shaking my hand and greeting me every Sunday influenced me more than he probably ever knew. I grew to consider Tony my buddy, even my friend at church. Tony helped me to see that men, real men, did attend church and profess Christianity. Tony recognized me, looked for me, and was glad to see me. To the other men in the church perhaps I may have been simply an annoying fat kid whose father rarely stepped foot in church. To Tony though, I was important.

Tony was not my mentor, nor did he disciple me, but he made me feel valued. He made me want to attend church, even in my teenage years. If I was not at church on Sunday, I knew Tony would miss me. Missing church meant the possibility of disappointing Tony and I did not want to do that. Tony makes it very near the top of the list of people most influential in shaping my life. In Tony's case, it simply meant knowing I existed. He was able to do that with a simple handshake and greeting every Sunday.

Well done: Ten keys to remaining faithful to the end

What about you? Are you a Tony to anyone? Are you purposely influencing others for the kingdom? Who could you be influencing for the kingdom? Like Tony, you may not even be aware your small acts of kindness are shaping lives for the better and for eternity. It does not take much to have great influence. Just a little effort on your part may make an eternal difference.

Whether you realize it or not, your sphere of influence is actually huge. You are influencing others far beyond your family or the church you attend. You influence people at work, in the checkout line, at your favorite restaurant, on social media, and even in traffic. We are all still human and haven't yet attained our goal of becoming like Christ, but our influence on others should be more constructive than destructive.

Jesus said we, as Christians, are the light of the world. Light attracts attention. Light shines on the good and the bad and can't go unnoticed or be ignored. Unless you are a completely stealth Christian and have hidden your light completely, you need to realize some people may base their opinion of God and

#3: Use your influence for the Kingdom

Christianity on you. As a Christian, you represent Christ. You are His ambassador. Good ambassadors cause those they encounter to think better of the one they represent. A poor ambassador can damage reputations. In the fifth chapter of Matthew, Jesus calls His followers the "light of the world." Being a good light, He says, means that what others see in us should bring glory to the Father, not damage His reputation.

Charles Spurgeon put it this way, "The Bible is not the light of the world, it is the light of the church. But, the world does not read the Bible, the world reads Christians! 'You are the light of the world'".[15]

People watch you wherever you go and whatever you do. You are always influencing others. Even when you would rather it did not, your light is shining. You are representing Christ in all you do.

According to the twelfth chapter of Hebrews, we are surrounded by a great cloud of witnesses, so we should be very careful how we live. Theses witnesses most likely those heroes of the faith listed in chapter eleven. Even so, this verse is a great reminder that we are always being observed.

Nonbelievers and less mature believers alike also watch you closely. They look to see how you react in difficult situations. Do you react in anger or with the love of Christ? Do you stand up for righteousness, or do you try to blend in with the culture around you? You may be the model of Christianity for which someone else has longed.

Realizing that you represent Christ in your workplace, family, traffic, or even sporting events should be very sobering. As first Peter 2:12 reminds us, "live such good lives among the pagans that, though they accuse you of doing wrong, they may see your good deeds and glorify God on the day he visits us."

Simply letting our lights shine and unintentionally influencing individuals for the kingdom is great, but God also calls us to be intentional in our influence. Tony Storment was very intentional. He sought me out each week to make contact. He could have hurried out of church trying to

#3: Use your influence for the Kingdom

beat the Sunday after-church-rush at a local restaurant, but he took the time to find me.

Small actions, like greeting someone at Church, or being an authentic Christian in the workplace, can widely impact the kingdom. We are all called to take small actions for the kingdom. We are also all called to larger, more deliberate actions. Taking efforts to intentionally influence others for Christ can change lives, and even the world.

In the New Testament, Barnabus provides an excellent example of someone who obeyed God and took intentional steps to influence others. Barnabus' obedience changed the world by encouraging and influencing Paul and also resulted in the penning of much of the New Testament. Granted, God will always accomplish His will; and if Barnabus had not been obedient, God would have certainly found someone else to fill the role. But because he was obedient, Barnabus probably makes it near the top of the list of those who had a significant influence on the Apostle Paul.

Well done: Ten keys to remaining faithful to the end

After his conversion to Christianity, the Apostle Paul had much in his past he regretted. By his own admission, he had dragged Christians out of their homes to be put on trial. He cast his vote to have many executed for following Christ. He watched the coats of those who angrily hurled jagged rocks at Stephen.

Paul's encounter with the risen Christ on the road to Damascus, completely changed his life. His new relationship with Christ placed him among those he had been determined to eradicate before his conversion. This placed Paul in a very awkward situation and created uncertainty among the local Christians.

Wisely, Paul didn't immediately return to Jerusalem after his conversion and begin "high-fiving" the leaders of the church. Instead, he left the scene for approximately three years. Paul tells us in his epistle to the Galatians that he spent some time in Arabia before heading back to Jerusalem. While we don't know for sure what Paul did for those three

#3: Use your influence for the Kingdom

years, we can certainly speculate he spent that time growing and maturing in his new faith.

When Paul decided to visit Jerusalem, perhaps to study with the other apostles, he likely reasoned three years would be enough time to let bygones be bygones. Yes, he had a past of violent aggression and murder, but now he was a new creation, the old had passed away.

Surprisingly for Paul, this was not the case. Rather than being welcomed with open arms, we read in the ninth chapter of Acts the apostles in Jerusalem were fearful and distrustful of the man they knew only as Saul. The wounds inflicted by Saul still oozed. They had not yet healed. Changing his name to Paul did not change what he had done. Simply claiming to be one of them did not make it so. Perhaps, they thought, he was trying to infiltrate the movement from the inside. Then, once he knew all those involved, Saul would have them all arrested and executed.

Paul's story could have ended there, but God had other plans and He used one man's sphere of influence to make things right. Among the believers in the Jerusalem congregation, only Barnabus was willing to trust Paul. Barnabus used his influence to introduce him to the other believers, including the Apostles. Through Barnabus' efforts, Paul gained acceptance as a believer himself. Barnabus' influence allowed Paul to share the remarkable story of his conversion and the complete transformation of his heart.

    Paul was a man of great intensity and it seems he did nothing half-heartedly. Whether it was hunting down Christians or convincing others that Christ was the only way, Paul had a habit of stirring up people and finding trouble. As C.T. Studd observed, *"he pretty well blew up every place he went to"*.[16] In Damascus, immediately after his conversion, Paul went to the Jewish synagogue and preached Jesus. In response, the Jews decided to kill him. Probably fearing for their own safety as well as Paul's, the believers in Damascus whisked him out of town. They had to lower him down the city wall in a basket during the dark of night to avoid detection.

#3: Use your influence for the Kingdom

After gaining the confidence of the disciples in Jerusalem, Paul once again started preaching the Gospel and debating the religious leaders. This roused the anger of the Jews, who once again decided to kill him.

Reading between the lines in Acts, it appears the persecution of the Christians had slowed somewhat before Paul returned to Jerusalem. After Paul stirred the nonbelieving Jews to anger, the leaders of the church in Jerusalem, most likely including some of the disciples, took an unusual action. They escorted Paul to the nearest seaport and put him on a ship to get him out of town. With the Jerusalem believers waving goodbye and breathing sighs of relief, Paul sailed back home to Tarsus.

As soon as Paul left the scene, "the church throughout Judea, Galilee and Samaria enjoyed a time of peace and was strengthened".[17] Paul is shipped back to Tarsus, the church flourishes, and we hear nothing more of him for six to seven years.

We can only speculate what Paul did during those silent years, but it's probably safe to assume he did little public preaching or debating. Every other time he had done so ended up with an angry mob trying to kill him and the fearful believers escorting him out of town. Since it seems Paul returned to his hometown of Tarsus and lived there quietly, he most likely spent his time in quiet contemplation, one-on-one conversations about the Gospel, and study rather than fiery, anger-rousing preaching.

Paul's story could have ended again, this time quietly in Tarsus. Perhaps he could have become a monk and studied day and night. But, as before, God had other plans and used the intentional actions and influence of Barnabus to help Paul fulfill his purpose.

As the leaders of the church in Jerusalem realized Christianity had expanded into other nearby areas, they decided to send Barnabus to assist the church in Antioch, located in what is now Turkey. Barnabus taught and exercised his spiritual gifts there to help Christians grow and mature. He was very successful in this endeavor but felt there was something else he must do. Barnabus, surely with the prompting of the Holy Spirit, decided it was time to

#3: Use your influence for the Kingdom

find Paul and help him begin the ministry to which God had called him.

Barnabus remembered saying goodbye to Paul several years earlier as the believers in Jerusalem put him on the boat and wished him well, as long as he stayed out of Jerusalem. Perhaps Barnabus knew Paul planned to stay in Tarsus, or perhaps he had stayed in touch. Regardless, Barnabus saddled up his donkey, or at least bought a new pair of sandals, and headed out to find and retrieve Paul in Tarsus, some 123 miles from Antioch.

Somehow, likely with the help of the Holy Spirit, Barnabus located Paul. After a brief reunion, Barnabas exercised his gifts of encouragement, influence, and persuasion to convince Paul to come to Antioch with him. How did Barnabus persuade him? Did it include the promise that he would not let the Christians in Antioch throw him out of town when he started preaching? We don't know, but Paul agreed and the two of them returned to Antioch. Both Paul and Barnabus spent a peaceful year ministering to the church there. No one tried to kill them and no one escorted either of them out of town.

When the time was right the church officially commissioned Paul and Barnabus as missionaries to spread the Gospel of Christ to the ends of the earth. Paul, the apostle to the gentiles, began the work God had set aside for him and Barnabus was at his side.

Paul took his commission seriously and true to his past, he stirred up trouble. As he recounted in the eleventh chapter of II Corinthians, his penchant for stirring people up resulted in his being flogged at least eight times, getting stoned at least once, going hungry, nearly drowning, facing severe cold, and many other hardships.[18] Tradition tells us Paul's passion eventually got him beheaded. Yet, the result of Paul taking his calling seriously was a world turned upside down for Christ.

However, Barnabus made this possible. He took a chance on the former persecutor and introduced him to the disciples. Barnabas took the harrowing journey from Antioch to Tarsus to find Paul and convince him to begin his ministry. Barnabus was essential to Paul's

#3: Use your influence for the Kingdom

story and, therefore, the New Testament. Think about your own sphere of influence. Is there someone to whom you could be a Barnabus? Who in your world needs your encouragement to do great things for the Lord?

Edward Kimball is another person whose sphere of influence was far greater than he could have ever realized. While not considered a household name, even in Christian circles, God used him greatly.

Edward was a kind man who cared greatly for the teenage boys who attended a Sunday school class he taught in Boston in the 1850s. He took particular interest in one seventeen-year-old boy who had recently moved into the city from rural Massachusetts. This young man had gone only to school through the 5th grade. He had difficulty reading and was unfamiliar with the Bible or the essentials of Christianity.

After instructing this young man for a few weeks in class, Edward decided to pay him a visit. Edward found Dwight working at his uncle's shoe store. There, Edward shared the love of God with Dwight and

Well done: Ten keys to remaining faithful to the end

on April 21, 1855, Dwight L. Moody gave his heart to Christ.

    Dwight L. Moody is a name most would recognize. He became a very effective evangelist and "was used by God to lead thousands of people to Christ."[19] Moody went on to found schools and a church and proclaimed the gospel to the world.

    In 1883, Moody conducted evangelistic meetings in England. These meetings were well attended, and many found faith in Jesus. Among the people who attended one of those meetings was a young man who professed himself a Christ follower, but he was at the time lukewarm, perhaps even backslidden.

    The young man listened intently to Moody. Moody's passion for the lost and his dedication to Christ struck a chord with this young man. The longer he listened, the more uncomfortable he became. The conviction of the Holy Spirit was strong. No longer would he be able to be a Christian on the sidelines. He had to get involved. He had to pursue Christ with all he had.

#3: Use your influence for the Kingdom

Attending that meeting ignited a fire in this young man and he was never the same. His tepid Christianity instantly gave way to a fiery faith that changed him and his life's focus. That young man was Charles T. Studd, and now you may better understand why he gave much of his inheritance to the Moody Bible Institute.

Barnabus had an impact far greater than he probably even imagined. So did Tony Storment and Edward Kimball. Who are you influencing for Christ? Who has God placed within your sphere of influence? Your children, grandchildren? Other family members? Your coworkers, neighbors, or friends? Strangers you meet through a chance encounter?

Barnabus helped change the world, though he probably did not understand his acts of obedience would have such a broad impact. Are you ready to change the world? Like Barnabus, you too can become a world changer. Your small intentional actions may have an impact far greater than you may realize, this side of heaven.

Well done: Ten keys to remaining faithful to the end

World changers know they are being watched at all times. They influence others unintentionally and take intentional actions when needed. World changers realize their most important task may be simply encouraging someone else to do what God has called them to do. Changing the world may mean sacrificing like Barnabus who embarked on a potentially perilous journey to find and influence Paul. It may mean sacrificing time, position, and lifestyle but the glory of God is a great reward.

How do you change the world? One life at a time. God may call you to bring dramatic change to the world yourself. Or He may call you to simply help someone else reach his or her potential. Either way, you are changing the world for Christ. And since you now realize your best days are still ahead because you will not let yourself be defined by your age, there is no reason you shouldn't start changing the world today. Regardless of your age, the time to start being a world changer is now.

#4

Never stop learning and growing

Therefore, with minds that are alert and fully sober, set your hope on the grace to be brought to you when Jesus Christ is revealed at his coming.

I Peter 1:13

#4: Never stop learning and growing

I have discovered, probably a little too late, that my brain is like a sponge. However, at my age my brain sponge is already saturated. I can pour more information into it, but when I do, other information seems to pour right out. If you will forgive me for using accounting terminology, my brain seems to follow the LIFO rule, last in, first out. I can easily recall useless, outdated information stored in my memory banks for years. Newer, more important, and useful information, not so much.

Silly similes aside, learning seems to become more difficult as we age. This is probably why God instructed the people of Israel to take His commandments seriously and to "impress them on your children".[20] Children's brains are like sponges that are still dry, ready to soak up whatever they can. However, in this same section in the sixth chapter of Deuteronomy, God also instructs adults to talk about His commandments "when you sit at home and when you walk along the road, when you lie down and when you get up. Tie them as symbols on your hands and

Well done: Ten keys to remaining faithful to the end

bind them to your foreheads. Write them on the doorframes of your houses and on your gates".[21]

    I have used memory aids for years. Sometimes, when I am just about to pull down the covers and get into bed, I will remember some important task I forgot that day. To ensure I remember to take out the trash, fill the car up with gas, or something equally important, I toss a shoe or other article of clothing onto the floor in my bedroom's doorway. That way, when I trip over an odd shoe or see a misplaced sock on the floor the next morning, I will instantly remember the task on my "to do" list.

    This method has become less effective as I have aged. Sometimes I can't remember why I threw a sock on the floor and just pick it up and throw it into the laundry basket. Sometimes it takes more than one reminder. While I can't be entirely sure, I think God was speaking to older adults when He told the Israelites to write His laws on their gates and door frames and to tie the proverbial string around their fingers.

#4: Never stop learning and growing

To be used of God, we must be ready. We can't lie around and let our brains turn to mush. We must continually refill our minds with new, relevant spiritual information. We should never stop learning. Granted, we may have to "learn" the same thing more than once as we age.

It is not enough however, to simply train our brains and ignore our bodies. Yes, we may have more aches and pains as we age, and it seems extra pounds are far easier to find than lose. Even so, we need to do our best to keep our bodies in tune and ready for whatever God calls us to do.

This topic brings us back to Caleb. Remember him? He was fit and ready for battle at the age of eighty-five. He kept himself mentally and physically fit as he waited for the time God's promise would be fulfilled. He did not sit around all day watching television or posting updates on social media while gorging himself on dates, figs, pomegranates, and honey. No, he did everything possible to ensure he would be ready for battle when the call came.

Imagine for a moment what a typical day might have been like for Caleb. Like the prophet Anna to whom Luke introduced us, getting out of bed some days may have been difficult. but, Caleb was a warrior; warriors, prophetesses, apostles, and everyone else God uses, must press on in spite of physical limitations. Being a devout Jew who wholeheartedly followed God, Caleb surely started each morning with prayer, even before rising out of bed. His first prayer in the morning may have been something like:

"'I am thankful before You, living and enduring King, for You have mercifully restored my soul within me.'[22] You restore my strength daily and have prepared me to do Your will. You are faithful in keeping your promises, even to a thousand generations. And, when the appointed day arrives, with your help O Lord, I will strike down the Anakites and possess the land you promised to me, and to my children, and to my children's children."

After focusing his mind on his Lord and his goal, Caleb probably spent some of the morning meditating and studying God's law delivered by Moses. To help

#4: Never stop learning and growing

him remember and keep his mind focused on the task at hand, he may have glanced down at the leather band tied to his left wrist. There scrawled into the leather, Caleb could make out most of the words of the Shema, "Hear, O Israel, the Lord our God, the Lord is one."[23]

After spending some time in prayer, meditation, and scripture learning, Caleb knew it was time to prepare for the most important task of his life. God had promised it, and he believed it. Realizing that today might be the day, Caleb ensured he was battle ready.

Next, Caleb stepped out of his tent into the early morning sun. Smoke wafted from several small fires surrounded by families completing their breakfast. Small children ran past, chasing a lamb that had escaped its enclosure. It was going to be a good day.

Caleb then unsheathed his trusty sword and checked the edge. It was still razor sharp. No need to sharpen it today. Tomorrow, for sure. He then grabbed an oily cloth and ran it quickly up and down the blade. He continued to polish it until it revealed a distorted image of himself.

Seeing his reflection caused Caleb to break out into a huge smile, albeit with a missing front tooth. That tooth was a casualty of an argument over the ownership of a goat several years earlier. He had lost a tooth but kept the goat. His challenger in that argument lost two teeth and claim to the goat.

Caleb continued staring at his sword as he recalled using it in battle many years earlier to help defeat the Amalekites. It was the same sword he used to coerce the cowardly spies into bringing back the bounty of the Promised Land. When the time came, Caleb knew his weapon of choice would still be as ready as he was.

Caleb then sheathed his sword and strapped it onto his waist. Confidently, he made his way into a large clearing between several tents. Then, with his still forceful voice, he beckoned, "Come! Let's go over our battle plans!"

Soon he was surrounded by the clan's best warriors. Caleb once again ensured all knew which

#4: Never stop learning and growing

city they would take first. Again, they strategized about the best way to stealthily approach and then conquer the entire area, town by town.

"Today might be the day," Caleb encouraged. "We have to be ready. Now, who is up for a lesson in battle today?"

Caleb unsheathed his sword and waved it in the air in front of him. He was ready to hone his own battle skills and, at the same time, teach a lesson or two to the youngsters. First, he sparred with his son Jesher, and then his son Hur, but they were old men and provided only a little challenge. Next, he took on his grandson Uri. Uri was younger and fit. It was a very tough match, but Caleb was victorious.

After displaying his battle skills, Caleb commended his progeny for their skill, but suggested they continue honing their technique, because, after all, they were beaten by an 85-year-old man.

Caleb once again reminded all who would listen that even at the age of 85, he was "as strong today as the day Moses sent me out. I'm just as vigorous to go out to battle now as I was then."[24]

Well done: Ten keys to remaining faithful to the end

Caleb put away his sword and stood at attention as he received the admiration he was due from the clan. Then he marched into his tent and took a short, but much deserved, pre-afternoon nap.

When the time came, Caleb was ready, but only because he kept his mind, body, and sword sharp. We must do the same. The apostle Paul and the author of the book of Hebrews, both compared the Christian walk to an athletic competition. We are told in several places to run the race to win, press on toward the goal, and to endure and persevere. In his first letter to the Corinthians, Paul told them:

> *Run in such a way as to get the prize. Everyone who competes in the games goes into strict training. They do it to get a crown that will not last; but we do it to get a crown that will last forever. Therefore, I do not run like someone running aimlessly; I do not fight like a boxer beating the air. No, I strike a blow to my body and make it my slave so that after I have preached to others, I myself will not be disqualified for the prize.*[25]

#4: Never stop learning and growing

You may recall that Paul suffered much physically and was probably in no condition to run marathons for pleasure. After being beaten and stoned more than once, and suffering a thorn in the flesh that may have been a physical aliment, he practiced self-discipline in an attempt to control both his body and mind. He was ready to do whatever God called him to do and kept pressing on to the goal of knowing and serving Christ.

We are each accountable for the blessings we have received. Perhaps you are blessed with good health. If so, thank God and vow to use that health to serve Him as long as you can. If you are not blessed with good health, don't think that disqualifies or excuses you from His service. A debilitating illness did not prevent Amy Carmichael from doing amazing things for Christ wherever she was, but especially in India.

Amy was born in Ireland in 1867. After coming to Christ, Amy, not well off herself, felt a call to minister to those less fortunate. As a young woman, Amy started teaching and ministering to poor women who worked in the local mill. They could not afford hats and so they covered their heads with shawls. These poor women in their cheap shawls were looked down on and felt unwelcomed in some churches. Amy moved into their neighborhood to be close to the poor women she ministered to. Before long, Amy's following had grown to more than 500. Needing a larger place to meet, Amy's ministry eventually erected a metal building that could comfortably hold 500 people. She named the building "Welcome Hall".[26]

Amy was not blessed with good health. She was afflicted with neuralgia, a painful nerve disease that resulted in her being bedridden for weeks at a time.[27] Despite her ill health, Amy felt God had bigger things in store for her. But, realizing God had great things in store for her did not deter her willingness to be used of God, wherever she was until she found her true calling.

After listening to a message by Hudson Taylor, a very successful pioneering missionary to China, Amy felt God calling her to the mission field. Friends laughed and told her this was impossible because of

#4: Never stop learning and growing

her ill health. Amy even trained with one mission society, but it determined she was unfit to serve because of her chronic illnesses. She was dismissed from that program.

Undaunted, Amy did not give up on her goal of becoming a missionary. Despite her ill health and rejection, Amy would not detour from pursuing that goal. She knew the mission field was where God was calling her. Her illness kept getting in the way. Recalling this, she once remarked, "What asses bodies are!"[28]

Eventually Amy found a mission society that would accept her. Still searching for her true calling, Amy traveled to Japan as a missionary. Perhaps, she thought, this is where God wanted her to serve. Japan did not agree with her. After 15 months, she became too ill to work there any longer and returned home, still determined she was destined to serve as a missionary.

Amy tried again. This time she ended up in what is now Sri Lanka, an island nation south of India. Again, she became ill. In 1895, Amy left Sri Lanka and traveled to Bangalore in southern India because of her health. Not surprisingly, this is exactly where God wanted her. He used Amy's illness to direct her to the work for which He had created her.

Soon after arriving in India, Amy became aware of the abhorrent practice of Hindu priests using young girls as prostitutes to fund and support their temples. These girls were often sold to the priests by their own parents or those pretending to be their parents. Sometimes these girls were born into the temple, their mothers being temple prostitutes themselves. Once they entered this life, these girls had no value in society, not even in their own families. Their future seemed bleak and inescapable. (Surprisingly, this practice still exists in some parts of India).

Horrified by this human trafficking and the terrible plight of these girls, Amy determined to do something. She began gathering up these young temple prostitutes to care for them. Before long, she was running a rescue center where she cared for and educated them. And, of course, she shared the Gospel with them.

#4: Never stop learning and growing

Word got out quickly. Before long, children were showing up at Amy's rescue center on their own, having escaped their abusers. Sometimes Amy kidnapped them from their abusers. To appear Indian, Amy would darken her skin and dress in traditional Indian clothing. The brown eyes she was born with became very useful in her stealthy rescue missions. Amy was even officially charged with kidnapping by the government of India, but those charges were eventually dismissed. Before long, Amy's rescue center was caring for over one thousand children, both girls and boys.

In her 60s in 1931, and still serving in India, Amy took a hard fall. Her injuries resulted in her being housebound and largely bedridden. While she could walk a few steps in great pain, Amy never regained her mobility. Yet, instead of giving up in despair, she continued to direct her ministry from her bedroom.

Amy also continued to write inspirational books. In the 20 years Amy was bedridden, she continued to serve her Lord with joy, published 16 books,[29] and oversaw her ministry. Amy was still ministering in India when she passed away at the age of 83. Once she arrived in India, she never left. She had found her true calling and worked at it with all she had.

Amy did not give up, even when her physical body did. She kept active mentally and spiritually. She kept her sword sharp. A few years after her injury, Amy penned these words:

> *It has been the custom of our Father to let us look into heaven while the fogs of earth are about us. It is then that the earthly ceases to dominate. We have seen something better than that. And deep in our happy hearts we know that all that grieves us is but for a moment, and all that pleases us is but for a moment, and only the eternal is important.*[30]

God uses people of all ages and in all physical conditions, as long as they are willing to be used. Even if you are not doing what you think is a great work for the Lord, you are still influencing others as His ambassador. Sometimes God uses people for great things when they are young and continues to use them

#4: Never stop learning and growing

throughout their lives. But in other cases, God's call may not come until the world has said we are too old to be useful.

Even if you are very limited in your physical abilities, God can still use you. If all you are able to do for Him is pray, then pray like no one else. As James tells us, the fervent prayers of the righteous accomplish great things. Perhaps you can send encouraging cards or emails from your sickbed. That may be exactly what God has called you to do. Be the best exhorter you can be, be a shining light to everyone in your sphere of influence in everything you do, well or ill.

If you feel God has more in store for you, keep pursuing it. But at the same time, don't quit doing what you are already doing for the Lord. He can and will use you right where you are. As He did with Amy Carmichael, God will lead you to the people and places He chooses.

In the small Bible school where I serve as director, most of our students are over the age of 50. Why are they there? They are sharpening their

Well done: Ten keys to remaining faithful to the end

swords, learning more so they can be ready for anything God may want them to accomplish, now or in the future.

Being willing to be used by God means keeping your mind and body in the best shape possible. Train both, exercising self-discipline even when it is not easy. Keep sharpening your sword.

Be sure also to continue nurturing your relationship with God. You can't be content with the same spiritual knowledge and relationship you had 10 years ago, last year, or even yesterday. Press on toward the goal of knowing Christ and being used by Him even more. Press on to gain the crown that will last forever.

#5

Don't give up before you're done

But as for you, be strong and do not give up,
for your work will be rewarded.
2 Chronicles 15:7

#5: Don't give up until you're done

At the time I am writing this, my friend Rick is a 68-year-old Vietnam veteran who does not quite look his age. In the little over three years I have known him, I have watched Rick purposely sharpen his spiritual weapons. He attends at least two weekly Bible studies and has attended classes at our small Bible school. He has a heart for the lost and desires greatly to help others find salvation in Christ.

Rick is a member of the small group my wife and I lead. We spend a good deal of time every week studying, sharing, and praying. Rick's requests for prayer almost always focus on his unsaved family members and a friend or two he is witnessing to. Rick often asks for boldness in communicating the gospel message to those he encounters.

Rick clearly loves his Lord, whom he did not meet until he was well into his forties. He also loves his wife to whom he has been married for over 20 years. He also loves his two children and his wife's son. If you ask, and even if you do not, Rick, or usually his wife, will quickly tell you that the two of them were supposed to be married many years earlier while they were still in their late teens. Rick though got cold feet and backed out shortly before the wedding day. Probably feeling a strong need to "get away", he joined the Army. When relating this part of their life story, Rick is quick to admit with an uneasy smile that he was guilty of leaving her at the altar.

    Some 20+ years later, Rick and his jilted would-be bride met again. At that time they were both recovering from failed marriages. They rekindled their friendship and were eventually married. There is substantially more to this part of Rick's story, but I will save that for an upcoming chapter.

    There is one other significant love in Rick's life: riding motorcycles. Rick rides his Indian motorcycle whenever he can. Snow and ice seem to be the only things that keep him in his cage, a biker's term for a car or truck. Rick likes to ride solo, in small groups, and in large groups. He likes short rides, long rides, and everything in between. He has crisscrossed the country several times on his motorcycle.

#5: Don't give up until you're done

Rick belongs to a motorcycle club that limits its membership to combat veterans. Most of the members are younger than Rick. And, as you might assume, these bikers are a bunch of rough and tough, hard-living, hard-riding, and hard-drinking individuals. Simply put, this is a group of unsaved souls who need someone to influence them positively, someone to show them The Light. These are just the type of people Jesus would hang out with and they are the people Rick is called to witness to.

A few weeks ago, at our small group meeting, Rick brought up a rare personal prayer request.

"I've been riding with these combat vets for a few years now," he began. "They're a pretty rough crowd. They all know I'm a believer, but I don't think I'm making a difference. I'm getting a little tired of the garbage, and I'm thinking about quitting this club. But I want to do what God wants, so please pray that He will give me direction."

We prayed that evening for Rick to have boldness and clarity.

Well done: Ten keys to remaining faithful to the end

Just a few weeks later we found out that God was not ready for Rick to end his association with this motorcycle club. It appeared God had more work for Rick to do with these needy souls.

In an update on his previous prayer request, Rick reported some very sad news. One of the members of the club took his own life the week prior. Rick had been witnessing to this individual and considered him a good friend. His death was very hard on Rick because, as far as he could tell, all his attempts to influence him for Christ had not made any difference.

"Oh, and I guess I'll be riding with this group for a while longer," Rick also reported. "Allen's suicide hit all of us pretty hard. A lot of the guys are thinking more about life and spiritual things. They've been asking me a lot of questions, and I'm doing pretty good at answering them with all the studying I've been doing and classes I've taken. I'm becoming bolder all the time. And they asked me this week to serve as the club's chaplain."

#5: Don't give up until you're done

Rick's reported answer to our prayers was met with smiles, light laughter, and someone in the group saying quietly, "Isn't it amazing how God works everything out."

God is not finished with Rick's influence in this group, even though Rick thought it was time to move on. I am excited to see how many members of this biker club Rick will positively influence with the Gospel. Rick could have given up. He was tired and had not seen any tangible results. But instead of just throwing in the towel on his own, he asked for God's direction.

Rick sought God's will as he continued to strive toward the goal of earning an eternal crown. When God made it clear it was not time to quit, Rick was faithful. Instead of affirming it was time to move on, God expanded Rick's influence with this group. Rick clearly learned that it's not over until God says it's over.

Sometimes God makes it very clear that our work for Him is complete. For example, tradition and early Christian writings tell us that Paul was beheaded in Rome. Tradition also tells us that all of the original disciples of Christ, except for John, were executed or murdered. God ended their ministry clearly and abruptly. There was no guessing when it was time to quit.

Even though the Apostle John lived to a very old age, he continued working for the Lord. John was far past normal retirement age when he compiled his apocalyptic Revelation, as he was commanded. Tradition tells us John continued to minister as long as he could. At a very old age, frail and weak, John was carried into the assembly of Christians in the arms of able bodied younger believers. Mustering all the strength he could, John weakly exhorted the believers to "love one another". He is reported to have done this in every gathering he attended.

Those in attendance grew tired of hearing the same command every time John appeared. Jerome reported that when John was asked why he only spoke this one command, he gathered enough strength to remind those in attendance this was the Lord's

#5: Don't give up until you're done

command and keeping it was more important than all else.[31]

Sometimes people give up on a task ordained by God before they should, especially when they make decisions without seeking God's advice, or refuse to submit to God's leading. The Old Testament book of II Kings illustrates this point very clearly with the story of two very different men, one godly and the other evil. The results are what you might expect. In chapter 13 of Second Kings, we read the story of Elisha, God's prophet, and Jehoash, the king of Israel.

By the time we read about Elisha in this chapter, he had already accomplished much after taking over from his mentor, Elijah. In his career as a prophet of God, Elisha had parted the Jordan River, made bad water good, cured a Syrian general's leprosy, raised a dead child, predicted the rise and fall of kings, predicted the outcome of battles, and performed many other miracles in the name of the Lord. Now, in this chapter we see him as a very old man, literally on his deathbed. Yet God was still not finished with him. He had one final task for Elisha.

Well done: Ten keys to remaining faithful to the end

Jehoash was the newly crowned king of Israel. As the text tells us, he did not make the list of good kings of Israel. Instead, the chapter tells us that Jehoash was an evil king. Even so, Jehoash understood the power Elisha had as a prophet of God. Military victories or losses, droughts or rainfall, famine or plenty, all seemed to stem from the proclamations of this prophet.

Hearing that Elisha was near death, Jehoash decided to pay him a visit. Perhaps he was seeking one last enduring blessing, some military council, victory over his enemies, or even to have Elisha bestow on him the power of a prophet. Perhaps Jehoash hoped Elisha would bequeath his cloak, or mantel, to him so he could be endowed with the power to conquer all who opposed him.

As Jehoash entered Elisha's home, imagine him scurrying into the prophet's bedroom. There he sees the old prophet lying in bed. Elisha is near death but still breathing. Jehoash's heart races. He has arrived in time to get what he wants from the elderly prophet.

#5: Don't give up until you're done

As the frail prophet wearily opens his eyes and looks up, Jehoash begins to speak.

"Elisha, you are like a father to me. Indeed, you are the father of Israel. I know that you are the true power in the nation. All of our soldiers and all of our chariots cannot succeed without your blessing."

Perhaps Jehoash was acknowledging that his reign as king, or even life, was contingent on God's approval. Or maybe he was just trying to flatter the prophet and soften his heart to get the old man ready for his request.

This passage also tells us that Jehoash wept over Elisha. Perhaps these were truly tears of sorrow for Elisha's condition. They also could have been tears that resulted from knowing his kingdom would not fare well without the prophet's blessing.

Before Jehoash could ask for an anointing of Elisha's power, the promise of victory, or even the tiniest of blessings, the prophet took over the conversation. Elisha, with God's power, knew what was in Jehoash's heart.

"Open that window over there," Elisha said with a shaky voice as he raised himself on one elbow and pointed to a window at the far side of the tiny room.

Jehoash was excited. Perhaps Elisha was summoning God's power through the open window. Excited by the possibilities, he moved quickly across the room, moved the shutter, and opened the window. Then, he turned to look at Elisha with great expectation. As he was about to ask for a blessing, Elisha again began to speak.

"Come back over here and bring your bow and all your arrows." Elisha's voice was louder. His strength was returning. He sensed God was giving him one more important task to perform before calling him home. Jehoash quickly followed the prophet's command and drew near with his bow and arrows.

Just a quick side note here, but I find it strange that the king of Israel carried weaponry. It seems that he would have people for that. But perhaps being a new king in a potentially tenuous reign, he may have traveled alone, perhaps even incognito. Perhaps he

#5: Don't give up until you're done

was ready for battle at all times. Regardless, he nocked an arrow and looked at Elisha.

Elisha then reached out his withered and wrinkled hand and touched the king's right hand as it held the notch of the arrow against the bow's string.

"Now," Elisha ordered, "shoot the arrow out the open window!"

Some Bible commentators report that in those days shooting an arrow in the direction of your enemy meant you were signaling your intention to battle and conquer them. Perhaps Jehoash studied from the same history books that these commentators did, or perhaps he simply thought Elisha's command somewhat odd. Regardless, Jehoash did as he was ordered and shot the arrow out the window.

"Excellent," Elisha proclaimed. "This is the Lord's arrow of victory! You will be completely victorious in your next battle against the Arameans."

Elisha was quick to explain that his power was not his own, but God's. Judging from his next actions, it appears Jehoash was not impressed with Elisha's pronouncement.

"Now take the rest of your arrows and hit the ground with them," Elisha commanded.

Some have interpreted Elisha telling Jehoash to strike the ground with the arrows to mean Elisha was instructing Jehoash to take the quiver full of arrows and bang it on the floor. Others have decided Elisha was telling Jehoash to continue to shoot the Lord's arrows of victory out the window until they hit the ground. Because it makes for a better story, I chose the "shoot the arrows" interpretation.

Let's assume that Jehoash agrees with my interpretation and shoots another arrow out the window and listens for it to strike the ground. Hearing the thud, he looks for approval from Elisha. Elisha says nothing. He remains motionless and expressionless.

Seeing no indication of approval or rejection from the prophet, Jehoash turns and shoots another arrow out the window. Feeling somewhat confused, Jehoash again glances at the prophet, hoping to see some indication that he is following orders correctly. But there is still no reaction from the prophet.

#5: Don't give up until you're done

Beginning to question the value of his trip to see the prophet, Jehoash slowly sets another arrow in the bow and fires it out the window. Once again he turns around, hoping for even the slightest reaction or indication from Elisha that he is on track.

Jehoash may have been one of those individuals who was motivated by praise. Or he may have suffered from an unhealthy self-image and needed continual feedback to know he was doing the right thing. Or he could have just been lazy.

Tiring quickly from this game of shooting arrows out the window, Jehoash lays his bow and arrows on the floor and looks at Elisha.

"Is that all you're good for?" Elisha asks loudly, becoming visibly angry. "Did I tell you to stop? No! Three lousy arrows! You've got a whole quiver full of arrows and you stopped after only three!"

Jehoash is dumbfounded. He received no clear instruction from Elisha. How did he know to keep going? It all seemed like a very silly game. A game with no rules.

"Because you stopped at three arrows," Elisha's voice is now quivering with anger. "You will have only three victories against the Arameans. You should have kept going to at least five or six, or until I told you to stop. But no, you're a quitter! You quit before you even got started."

After chiding Jehoash, Elisha was done -- completely. He had spent every arrow is his life's quiver. After relaying the story of Jehoash's half-hearted attempts at archery and Elisha's resulting anger, the very next verse in this chapter says, "Elisha died and was buried".[32]

Jehoash provides an excellent example of what we shouldn't do. If God has given us a task, we shouldn't, like Jehoash, decide we have had enough on our own. We shouldn't pursue our God-given tasks half-heartedly, even if we don't have clear direction. If we still have arrows in our quivers, we should continue to shoot them.

When wondering if our task is done, we should be like Rick when he faced uncertainty about his involvement with the motorcycle club. Ask the Lord if

#5: Don't give up until you're done

you have fired enough arrows or should keep firing. Jehoash never asked. He assumed he had done enough. He just decided on his own he had worked hard enough.

Erwin McManus, in his inspirational book "The Last Arrow", concludes a discussion of Jehoash and Elisha this way: *We are not supposed to die with our quivers full. In fact, our greater aspiration should be to die with our quivers empty".*[33]

What about you? Will you end your life with a full or empty quiver? Are you seeking to end your task or ministry before it is finished? Or are you, like Elisha, anticipating being used of God, even until the day you die?

Your work for the Lord, whatever it may be, is not done until He says so.

#6

Learn from your past mistakes

*But it is the spirit in a person,
the breath of the Almighty, that gives them
understanding. It is not only the old who are wise,
not only the aged who understand what is right.
Job 32: 8 – 9*

#6: Learn from your past mistakes

Do you remember when you knew everything? If you are normal, then you probably thought just that in your teenage years. Most teens think they know everything and are sure they are far more intelligent and wiser than their any adult in authority. Most people outgrow this attitude and return to reality once they reach their mid-twenties. For others, maturity takes a little longer. I probably fit into this category since I seem to have to "learn" the same lessons repeatedly, and I am a late bloomer.

Take a quick inventory of your own life, from your teenage years to now. As you look back, have you grown wiser? Certainly, knowing what you now know, you would have done things differently than you did when you were younger. For example, would you have still gotten that tattoo, attended that party, experimented with controlled substances, quit that job, delayed going to college, talked back to your parents, stopped attending church, avoided visiting

Well done: Ten keys to remaining faithful to the end

your grandparents, or made any number of bad decisions?

The more time between now and your teen years, the broader the gap you may notice between the foolishness of your youth and the wisdom you have today. Hopefully.

All this introspection and examination of your past could have one negative impact. You may determine your past actions and decisions were even more foolish than you realized. Don't dwell on your past. Take Paul's advice. Forget the past and press forward. Also take comfort in the fact that you realize the folly of your past when you contrast it with where you are today.

For most people, it is logical to assume that their age and level of wisdom are positively correlated. That is, the older they are, the wiser they become. However, wisdom is not limited to those approaching or in retirement. You may occasionally find younger people who seem to possess a great deal of wisdom. We say those individuals are "wise beyond their years".

#6: Learn from your past mistakes

Yet, the process of aging itself does not make us wiser. You can probably think of people older than you but are not wise, perhaps even foolish. There are people who are old enough to have gained wisdom, but somehow failed to do so. We might say they are "foolish despite their years". Strong words yes, but the Bible seems to support this.

The process of aging can make us wiser, but only if we learn from our mistakes. When you were younger, you likely tried things that did not end up as you dad hoped. For example, maybe your entire retirement plan consisted of hoping to win the lottery. As retirement became something you could actually see occurring, you hopefully learned the folly of your previous plan and began saving. Better late than never. Our past mistakes should lead us to better decisions. That is what sets the wise apart from the foolish.

Some people, both old and young, refuse to learn from their mistakes and, therefore, never become wise. They make the same foolish decisions again and again. They suffer the consequences of their foolishness repeatedly but refuse to change. The book of Proverbs relates several examples to drive this point home. One of those says, "Whoever loves discipline loves knowledge, but whoever hates correction is stupid".[34] These are God's words, not mine.

As this proverb suggests, learning can sometimes be painful. My wife Tracy has a favorite expression, "Some people learn by instruction, and others learn by correction." Learning by correction can be painful --literally. Think back to some of the painful lessons you learned over the course of your life. For example, you may have learned from experience not to; touch a hot stove, stick your hand in a pan of boiling water, play with fishing lures, play with staplers, or use a cheap step stool to hang Christmas decorations. The step stool lesson was particularly painful for me and resulted in four fractured vertebrae.

No matter how "wise" we are, we all continue to slip into foolishness now and then. Even though we know better, we can still make the same mistakes. For example, even knowing the result, do you still fall into

#6: Learn from your past mistakes

the trap of saying hurtful things to those you love when you are angry? Do you spend too much time watching television? Do you still spend too much money eating out? Do you still continue to eat pastries and ice cream when you should be losing weight? Do you waste hours playing games when you could instead be sharpening your spiritual weapons? This is my list. Yours may be different and, hopefully, shorter.

    The good news is we can gain wisdom as we age, if we learn from our past mistakes. We are not yet perfect. Remember, not even the Apostle Paul had attained his goal of perfection. But, the wise person keeps striving, keeps trying to learn from his or her mistakes, and keeps trying to avoid stupidity.

    As I have matured, I have learned many painful lessons resulting from my tendencies toward arrogance and pride. Proverbs 18:2 seems to be written specifically for me. This verse states, "Fools find no pleasure in understanding but delight in airing their own opinions."

Well done: Ten keys to remaining faithful to the end

    I had been instructing adults for over 30 years and was in my early 50s when my wife Tracy encouraged me to further my education. I already had a master's degree and was sure I knew everything there was to know about my areas of expertise, teaching adults and software applications. But wanting to please my wife and because I was a little bored, I enrolled in a doctoral program. I selected a field I was sure would be easy: one in which I was confident I could pass every test without even having to open a book. I chose to focus on adult education and leadership.

    As I applied for acceptance into this degree program, I was confident that completing it would be fast and relatively painless. After all, I already knew all there was to know about this topic.

    In reality, only one thing about earning this degree came quickly, and it was also very painful. I learned within a few minutes of my first class that I did not know everything. It was a significant blow to my ego.

#6: Learn from your past mistakes

The good news is I recovered from this indignation and humbled myself to become a learner. From then on, I enjoyed my courses greatly and learned more than I ever thought possible. I also learned how much I did not know. I learned there are libraries filled with information I will never know.

When it came to knowledge of the Bible, I was also fairly arrogant. I had been teaching adult Bible classes for many years when Tracy and I married. (You may recall it is Tracy who has the master's degree in theology.) Our heated theological and Bible discussions began even before we were married. We both come from different schools of thought on some of the nonessentials of Christianity. In the course of those "discussions", I came to realize how much I did not know about the Bible and theology. Again, realizing I did not know everything put me in the position to learn. But, getting to that point was often very painful.

I think realizing we don't know everything is the first step to gaining wisdom. Unrepentant arrogance and an unteachable spirit will never lead to wisdom, instead it keeps us foolish despite our years.

As I was considering biblical examples of individuals who gained wisdom by learning from their mistakes, I was reminded of Moses. In the second chapter of Exodus we learn Moses was raised in Pharaoh's palace. Even so, he was significantly influenced by his Hebrew mother, who was able to remain part of his life, especially when he was very young. Despite his status as an adopted grandson of Pharaoh, Moses still knew he was a Hebrew and that they were his true people.

One day, as an impulsive young man of 45 years old, Moses ventured out of the palace to hang out with his kinsmen. Stephen's speech in the seventh chapter of Acts tells us Moses was beginning to realize he had been called by God to rescue his people from bondage and lead them to the Promised Land. Even so, it would appear that Moses had not yet learned to work under God's direction. It also seems he was prone to taking matters into his own hands.

#6: Learn from your past mistakes

While on this particular outing, described in the second chapter of Exodus, Moses observed the suffering and mistreatment of his fellow Jews at the hands of their Egyptian task masters. Certainly, his mother had told him about Pharaoh's order to throw all male Jewish babies into the Nile River. The story of this attempted genocide may have been in his mind as he watched his people suffering as Egypt slaves.

As Moses witnessed the slavery and oppression first hand, he saw a terrible injustice: an Egyptian brutally beating a Hebrew slave. This horrendous cruelty probably caused the anger within him to reach a boiling point. He vowed to himself that this act would be punished. Something must be done to avenge his kinsman! This Egyptian could not be allowed to get away with this evil. God needed to act immediately to avenge this injustice.

In his anger, it seems Moses decided God needed some help in punishing this Egyptian. He then made a very rash and foolish decision. Instead of waiting for God's timing to avenge this beating, free the Hebrews, and lead them to their homeland, Moses decided it was time to act, on his own, without God's direction or assistance.

When no one was looking, or so he thought, Moses gave the Egyptian what he thought he deserved. Moses beat the Egyptian, as he had beat the Hebrew slave. But Moses did not stop the beat-down until the cruel taskmaster was dead. To hide the evidence, Moses buried the Egyptian's body in the sand. Moses was sure he had struck the first blow in the fight for Hebrew freedom. It seemed like a good idea at the time.

Yielding to his anger and acting on his own resulted in Moses committing murder or depending on which commentaries you read, at least committing a justifiable vengeful killing. Regardless, Moses acted on his own and did not wait for God's timing. Moses also exhibited a lack of faith in God's ability to avenge His chosen people. God reminded Moses again that vengeance was His prerogative clearly when He later said, "It is mine to avenge; I will repay. In due time their foot will slip; their day of disaster is near and their doom rushes upon them."[35] Moses set himself

#6: Learn from your past mistakes

up for a long lesson in patience and gaining faith because of his foolish decision.

Moses thought his crime was hidden, but soon realized to his horror that his actions had been observed. News of Moses' actions quickly went viral. In no time at all, it was the talk of the palace and even Pharaoh found out. There was only one proper course of action for Pharaoh to take. Moses must be executed.

Moses, not quite ready to die a martyr, left town. For the next forty years he cared for sheep, raised a family, and learned patience. During his time in Midian, Moses also encountered the Living God and had a chance to grow in his faith. As he aged and learned, he also grew wiser during his time of exile.

When God deemed the time right, Moses returned to Egypt. God also confirmed to Moses that he was indeed the one who would lead the Hebrews to freedom. God promised Moses he would not be acting on his own. He would be acting for God, with His direction, and in His power.

After he returned to Egypt, Moses confronted a new Pharaoh and demanded he let the Hebrews go.

Well done: Ten keys to remaining faithful to the end

Pharaoh was not accustomed to having other people tell him what to do and quickly put up his defenses. Pharaoh responded to Moses by essentially saying, "You're not the boss of me, and neither is your puny god."

Pharaoh refused Moses' request, just as God said he would. He also mocked Moses and the miracles he and his brother Aaron performed at God's command.

Even though God had explained that Pharaoh would not be easy to deal with, I can imagine Pharaoh's rebuke stung Moses. It likely rekindled the Moses' famous temper. However, while he may have been tempted to drag Pharaoh out behind a pyramid and teach him a permanent lesson, this time Moses trusted the Lord to avenge His people. After all, Moses had taken matters into his own hands once before and that did not work out so well.

Moses returned to Egypt wiser than when he left because he learned from his past transgressions. He had also encountered and learned to trust God.

#6: Learn from your past mistakes

As I mentioned earlier, possessing wisdom does not mean attaining perfection. We may struggle with the same issues well into our dotage. We may have already learned the folly of some decisions and actions, yet, because we are human, fall into the same traps.

Moses was no exception. He was an imperfect human. Clearly, two of the major issues he had to overcome were unbridled anger and limited faith. Both of these were certainly involved in his killing of the Egyptian taskmaster. Scripture indicates these two traits of his humanity also followed Moses into his senior years.

In the twentieth chapter of Numbers we see Moses falling back into his old habits. This incident occurs after the spies return from the Promised Land. You will recall the Israelites angered God because of their lack of faith. They listened to the cowardly spies rather than to Caleb and Joshua. In the incident recorded in this chapter, we see the people once again complaining, something they apparently did with regularity.

Well done: Ten keys to remaining faithful to the end

    The Hebrews once again lament leaving Egypt and again complain Moses is a terrible leader who wants them all to die. They complain about blowing dust, scorching heat, improper sanitation facilities, significant stench, boring food, and not having enough water to drink. They complain about everything.

    Moses, as was his custom after listening to the people whine, pleaded with God to intervene. Fed up with their griping, Moses may have even complained a little himself while seeking God's guidance. We are not told exactly what he said this time, but the eleventh chapter of Numbers recorded this from Moses during another, similar event:

> *"Why have you brought this trouble on your servant? What have I done to displease you that you put the burden of all these people on me? Did I conceive all these people? Did I give them birth? Why do you tell me to carry them in my arms, as a nurse carries an infant, to the land you promised on oath to their ancestors? Where can I get meat for all these people? They keep wailing to me, 'Give us meat to eat!' I cannot*

#6: Learn from your past mistakes

> *carry all these people by myself; the burden is too heavy for me. If this is how you are going to treat me, please go ahead and kill me—if I have found favor in your eyes—and do not let me face my own ruin."*[36]

As is the Lord's custom, He answered Moses and promised He would provide water. The Lord instructed Moses to speak to a rock and, as he did, water would instantly begin flowing from it. Moses listened to God's instructions, yet for some reason, once again, took matters into his own hands.

Moses may have still been angry with the people when he left the meeting tent. He may have even been a little angry with God for giving him such an impudent bunch of complainers to lead around. Perhaps it was anger that caused Moses to ignore God's instructions. Maybe he just did not listen carefully. Or maybe he thought God needed a little help.

Instead of speaking to the rock, Moses struck the rock in anger as he scolded the Israelites. Moses also took credit for having a spring spout from the rock instead of giving God the glory. In chiding the Hebrews, he essentially said, "Listen here you bunch of miscreants! Do I have to do everything for you?"

Even in his old age, Moses reverted into his old ways. He let his temper and lack of faith rule the day. God was, understandably unhappy. Moses should have known better. Because of this foolish decision, Moses lost his chance to enter the Promised Land. His eternal salvation was not in danger, but he still suffered the consequences of his lack of wisdom and self-control.

As you mull over your own path to gaining wisdom, consider one more biblical example. In the twelfth chapter of I Kings we see a very sharp contrast between the wisdom gained through age and experience and the rashness of youth.

Rehoboam inherited the united kingdom of Israel from his father Solomon. As he took the throne, one of the most pressing things he needed to deal with was the considerable discontentment and frustration in the land. His father Solomon imposed exorbitant taxes and a policy of forced labor on the people to

#6: Learn from your past mistakes

support his many wives and concubines. Solomon wanted bigger and better houses and saw it as the duty of his subjects to provide for his wants. The northern portion of the country was especially resentful of his tax policy because they received little, if any, benefit from Solomon's lavish expenditures.

    Rehoboam knew he must deal with this issue or face the risk of losing the throne and the kingdom. First, he sought counsel from some of Solomon's advisors who were still on staff at the palace. These wise elders encouraged Rehoboam to extend an olive branch to the people. He should, they suggested, affirm that he would be a king that would look out for their interests and reduce their burdensome taxes. This, they advised, would strengthen the kingdom and keep the northern tribes forever loyal to him.

    Not yet very wise himself, Rehoboam decided to get a second opinion. He called together a group of his friends and asked them what they would suggest he do. The passage in I Kings tells us these individuals grew up with Rehoboam, and were likely close to his age. The passage also contrasts these from the elders by calling them young men. So, in other words, the impetuous young king rejected the advice of the older, wiser counselors and asked his drinking buddies for their recommendation.

Rehoboam's friends suggested he lay down the law. Rule with an iron fist. They told him to be even harder on the people than his father had been. That was the best way, they advised, for him to hold on to his throne and gain their respect. He needed to show them who was boss.

Rather than heeding his father Solomon's words recorded in Proverbs, "Fools give full vent to their rage, but the wise bring calm in the end[37]," Rehoboam found the "advice" of his friends more attractive. It appealed to his ego.

It was settled then. Rehoboam would try tyranny. Rehoboam responded to the northern tribes' delegation with, "If you think my father was bad, just wait until you see how I treat you. My father treated you far too kindly! He was a wimp. There's a new king on the throne and I'm bigger and badder than my dad ever was!"

#6: Learn from your past mistakes

Rehoboam's response was not what the delegation from the frustrated, over-taxed northern tribes expected to hear from their new king. They didn't take Rehoboam's arrogance well at all. They informed Rehoboam they no longer considered him their king, wished him well, and stormed off to choose another king for their territories. The result of Rehoboam's rejection of the wise counsel of the older men was the eventual division of the kingdom. Ten of Israel's 12 tribes abandoned Rehaboam and established the northern kingdom.

If you are reading this book, it is a good assumption you, left to your natural hair color, have at least a few strands of gray or you are probably reading this with someone older in mind. Regardless of your age, if you have learned from your mistakes, you are gaining wisdom. If you are someone who learns from correction, then rejoice that you have left a trail of mistakes and disasters in your past. Consider all your previous blunders as opportunities to gain additional wisdom.

Well done: Ten keys to remaining faithful to the end

Age, and the wisdom it helps us gain, can be a blessing, not only to ourselves but to others. So, what do you do with all the wisdom you have attained over the years to help others? Share it, but with humility. Mentor those in your sphere of influence, officially and unofficially. Take a younger person to lunch. Teach a class at church. Lead a Bible study in a small group. Share your story and be sure to include some of your "wisdom-gaining opportunities". Be a friend to those who need one. Counsel those who seek your advice.

Realize that no matter how wise you are, some people will refuse to heed your advice. Just as Rehoboam rejected the wise advice of the elders, others will reject your sage advice, as well. Don't get too offended when that happens. Realize that individual is still in the process of learning wisdom the hard way, just as you had to learn some hard lessons yourself.

When someone refuses to take your brilliant advice, it may be tempting to quickly come in with "I told you so" when disaster strikes. However, that may not be wise. We are not told in scripture if any of the

#6: Learn from your past mistakes

elders who correctly counseled Rehoboam later reminded him of their suggestion when the kingdom began to fall apart. Doing so may have proved very costly, maybe even deadly. In your case, reminding a foolish friend of the wise counsel you provided may cost you a friendship, resulting in your losing important influence with that individual.

As with everything in our journey of becoming more like Christ, we can't rest and think we are wise enough. Left to our own inclinations, we will revert to foolishness, just as Moses did. Thank God for the wisdom you have gained and ask Him to continue to guide you into more wisdom so that you can continue to be used by Him. Remember also that "If any of you lacks wisdom, you should ask God, who gives generously to all without finding fault, and it will be given to you."[38]

As you leave this chapter pondering wisdom, consider one final biblical exhortation:

> *Get wisdom. Though it cost all you have, get understanding. Cherish her, and she will exalt you; embrace her, and she will honor you. She*

Well done: Ten keys to remaining faithful to the end

> *will give you a garland to grace your head and present you with a glorious crown.*[39]

#7

Take charge of your time, energy, and finances

*The seed that fell among thorns stands for those who
hear, but as they go on their way
they are choked by life's worries, riches and pleasures,
and they do not mature.*
Luke 8:14

#7: Take charge of your time, energy, and finances

If you are a parent or have been around small children at all, you know raising them is not for the faint-hearted. Raising children zaps the life out of all who attempt it. It often seems every minute of every day, and every dollar you have and then some, are sucked from you in the child-rearing process. When raising children, it seems sometimes that is all you are doing. There is little, if any, time for anything else.

Of course, children are a blessing from the Lord. But, sometimes that is hard to remember when you are in the midst of child-rearing. The point I am making is that the process of raising children of all ages can be time consuming and, to further make the point of this chapter, ministry limiting.

Having children in the home does not mean you won't have other spheres of influence. We are all given spiritual gifts for the edification of the Body of Christ. Raising children does not give you a pass from other forms of ministry. It is just that, done correctly, ministering to your children, along with your relationship with God and your spouse, should be your highest priorities, not to the exclusion of other ministries, but certainly at the forefront.

It is likely your children are long beyond that stage, and perhaps you realize you could have done more to influence them for God. If this is the case, do what Paul encouraged, forget the past, and press on toward the goal. God's grace is sufficient in all things.

Consider how much additional free time you have now that the days of small children running around constantly screaming "mommy" or "daddy" are long past. Now, think back to when you began your work life. Perhaps you, as I did, attended college while working and raising a family. Perhaps you worked tediously to gain those promotions and get ahead. Perhaps you clawed up the workplace ladder. If that was the case, every minute you did not spend with your family was probably spent working or studying. Or perhaps you worked in an hourly job that let you have some time at home, but your job spent all your physical energy, leaving little for anything else.

#7: Take charge of your time, energy, and finances

By now, you should realize that even though aging presents its own set of challenges, there are many time-consuming challenges you may no longer face.

Yes, you may still deal with children. If you are a grandparent those visits and babysitting requests tap your time, strength, and patience, but the little blessings go home, eventually. Then, after you have spent a few hours repairing, cleaning, and putting away everything they touched, your time is spent how you choose to spend it.

Consider your profession. If you are currently retired, work is a memory. Hopefully a pleasant one. If you are nearing retirement, you have likely already reached the pinnacle of your career. Pre-retirement years are often spent planning for the future and the strong desire for career progression usually diminishes. Retired or not yet retired, your career probably takes less of your time and mental energy than it did when you were younger.

Don't forget that you are likely in a better position to be used by God right now than ever before.

Well done: Ten keys to remaining faithful to the end

Think about it. You are probably more secure financially than you have been in the past. More of your time is discretionary. It may seem you are constantly busy, and you probably are. But look closely at how you spend your time. You will likely find much more of your time is spent on your preferences, rather than necessities. The same is likely also true with your finances.

You may not agree but consider this. I haven't yet reached retirement and am certainly looking forward to the day I no longer have to punch a time clock. However, I do have many friends and acquaintances who are already retired. Many of them, especially those who are newly retired, have expressed a similar complaint. They are just too busy now that they're retired. Many remark they have no idea how they got anything done when they still had a job. By the time they go to the gym, visit the doctor, drop by the post office, have lunch, and then pick up a few groceries for dinner, the day is gone. There is no time for ministry, sword sharpening, or anything else important or edifying.

#7: Take charge of your time, energy, and finances

If you can relate to the previous paragraph, then you need to be introduced to Parkinson's Law. This law states that "work expands so as to fill the time available for its completion."[40] Simply put, if you have all day to visit the gym, doctor, post office, and grocery store, it will take all day. If you had only half a day to accomplish all those tasks, or just a few hours, the odds are pretty good you could do it. My friend and colleague, Dr. Brett Morris, shared something he learned early in his distinguished career as a colonel in the US Air Force. In a perfect illustration of Parkinson's Law, his rule in assigning work was, "If you want to get something done, give it to a busy person."

I have experienced this law myself. Being college faculty for a few years, I had summers off. It was much like retirement, but only for a few months. I always began my summer breaks with great plans. I would exercise more, work on the yard, plant a garden, read a few books, or write a book. But after I went fishing a few times, rode my motorcycle occasionally, drove around from store to store looking for gardening ideas, and went camping a couple of times, the summer was over. It was time to go back to work without accomplishing many of my goals.

I also experienced something else. Once I reentered the structure of the workday, I was able to accomplish much more. I approached the summer knowing I had plenty of time to accomplish my goals and consequently wasted time because I had it in abundance.

Being a good steward also means managing our time. Paul exhorts us in Ephesians to "Be very careful then how you live – not as unwise but as wise, making the most of every opportunity because the days are evil."[41] Paul knew that using our time wisely, like every other aspect of our lives, takes discipline. Realizing that you are in control over how you choose to spend your time is the first step in "making the most of every opportunity". If you are still working, then you realize even more the importance of practicing good stewardship over your time.

At this time in your life, you should have more time than ever to serve the Lord. If not, you may need

#7: Take charge of your time, energy, and finances

to learn better time management. Freeing up time means being able to prioritize tasks and activities.

We can also find ourselves spending significant amounts of our time in tasks that seem important but do little to help us accomplish our goals. Sometimes we get involved with tasks that neither serve the Kingdom well nor are personally fulfilling or edifying. But, these tasks can often seem important and perhaps we found it difficult to say "no". We can also get tunnel vision and think we are the only ones who can accomplish those tasks.

As you are evaluating what you are currently doing and could be doing for Kingdom service, you may need to establish or at least rearrange your priorities. Rather than getting bogged down in the mundane, prioritizing your tasks and assignments may help you see past the immediate demands on your time.

One of the best biblical examples of someone learning to prioritize tasks and free up time to focus on God's best is Moses. Studying the life of Moses can actually be very encouraging. The Bible records him as a great leader, hero of the faith, one who talked with God, delivered His law, and wrote several books of the Old Testament. Yet, the Bible also records his humanity and shows the mistakes he made and the lessons he learned.

In the eighteenth chapter of Exodus we read about Moses being very busy with what he thought was the most important thing he could do. Moses also suffered from tunnel vision, and thought he was the only one that could accomplish what he was doing.

Moses spent his entire day judging disputes between the people he led out of Egypt. These people, as we already know, had many complaints, and apparently many disputes, with their neighbors and probably their in-laws, too. From dawn to dusk, Moses listened to each side of the argument and then ruled in favor of the right side or gave advice for settling the dispute. Moses thought he was acting according to the Lord's will and thought he was doing the best he could.

As Moses was spending his days doing nothing but mediating and judging, his father-in-law Jethro

#7: Take charge of your time, energy, and finances

paid him a visit. Jethro was amazed as he observed the long lines of people waiting to have their case heard. He also saw Moses carefully listening to both sides of the case, taking time to deliberate and then issue his ruling. This left Moses no quality time for his family or to enhance his relationship with the Lord.

"Moses," Jethro said as he vied for Moses' attention between cases. "What in the world are you doing?"

"Judging the disputes between the people. I'm ruling in their cases as the Lord would have me." Moses saw nothing wrong with what he was doing.

"Son, I've known you for some forty years now, right?" Jethro paused for a moment to make sure Moses was listening. He also wanted to be sure Moses remembered their family relationship.

"Of course," Moses replied, still suspecting nothing was amiss.

"Okay then," Jethro continued, now that he knew he had Moses' attention. "I say this with all due respect, but you're not being very smart here. In fact, this is just plain dumb."

"Huh?" The anger began to burn a little in Moses, but he decided to give his father-in-law a hearing before having the bailiffs forcibly remove him from the court. Jethro was family and that meant he was due the respect of having his opinion heard.

"You're just getting worn out and the line of people is getting longer every day. It's taking you forever to hear one case at a time. It won't be long before they once again turn on you and demand that you resign. Or they may just drag you out into the desert and be done with you once and for all."

"So, what should I do?" Moses signaled he was willing to learn. Scripture shows us Moses was willing to learn from his mistakes.

Jethro then helped Moses prioritize and delegate. He told Moses that other godly men could hear cases and that would free him up to work on more important tasks. Wisely, Moses followed Jethro's advice and people's court began.

Once Moses was free of the entanglement of the busyness of hearing disputes, he was able to turn his attention to the very important things God had in

#7: Take charge of your time, energy, and finances

store. It was not until after Moses made the decision to free up his time that he ascended Mount Sinai and received the Ten Commandments and other instructions from the Lord. In working hard, but not managing his time well, Moses was delaying God's real call.

If you are maturing in age, God has placed you in a perfect place to be used of Him. The demands on your time, if you honestly examine them, should be less than at other times in your life. Your finances are likely more stable. However, you may need to do some rearranging of both to allow God to use you even more.

The Bible contains other illustrations to show us the importance of prioritizing how we spend our time, money, and energy. For example, in addition to comparing the Christian walk to athletic competitions, Paul also occasionally compared it to the life of a soldier. In stressing the need for full commitment to Christ, he reminded, "No one serving as a soldier gets entangled in civilian affairs, but rather tries to please his commanding officer."[42]

Well done: Ten keys to remaining faithful to the end

In this passage, Paul makes the point that anything that detracts from following Christ wholeheartedly is an entanglement. For a soldier, civilian affairs are not evil, but they are a distraction. Worrying about getting the crops harvested, ensuring little Augustus gets to gladiator practice on time, or being a campaign volunteer for a law and order candidate for the senate are not bad things. But for a soldier, they distract and entangle. They erode performance and take a soldier's head out of the game. This is no different with following Christ. Anything that entangles or even distracts us from complete devotion to Christ does not please our commanding officer. As Jesus explained in the parable of the sower, the cares of this world can easily entangle our lives and limit our effectiveness for Him.

    Without rehashing the entire second chapter of this book, let me just remind you that things of this world can be blessings from God. And, yes, those blessings will demand your time and attention. And, no, I am not encouraging anyone to give their children up for adoption or sell all they have to become less

#7: Take charge of your time, energy, and finances

entangled. But if you are voluntarily entangling yourself in things that do detract from the best God has in store, it may be time for an honest evaluation.

If you want to be fully used of God, now is probably the best time in your life for that to happen. Pray earnestly about what you are currently doing for God, your church, your family, and your friends. Ask God to show you if you have become entangled in doing good things when you could be doing great things for Him.

As an unentangled retired, or soon to be retired, individual, your options for pursuing God's kingdom are only limited by your imagination. You could start a neighborhood Bible study, organize service projects, participate in short-term mission trips, or volunteer at a soup kitchen. You can also use your unentangled time to pray, sharpen your spiritual weapons, and nurture your relationship with Christ.

Take charge of your time, money, and energy. Use them to pursue your goal of knowing and becoming more like Christ. Unentangle your life and serve Him wholeheartedly. Run the race with gusto!

#8

Learn from the Lord's discipline

I would go to the deeps a hundred times to cheer a downcast spirit. It is good for me to have been afflicted, that I might know how to speak a word in season to one that is weary.
Charles Spurgeon

#8: Learn from the Lord's discipline

Charles Spurgeon preached his first sermon when he was only 16 years old. In 1854, at the age of 19, he was hired as the senior pastor of the largest Baptist church in London. His reputation as a preacher quickly grew, and people came in droves to hear this dynamic young man. The swell of attendees created challenges for his church. After twice outgrowing its facilities, the church undertook the building of Metropolitan Tabernacle. When complete, it would hold six thousand people. Spurgeon could be considered to have started the first modern megachurch.[43]

While the Metropolitan Tabernacle was being built, Spurgeon held services in the Surrey Gardens Music Hall. In those evening services, Spurgeon routinely filled the hall with over 10,000 people, who came to hear the gospel preached.

One evening, just a few minutes after the service began, someone yelled, "Fire!" Panicked, members of the audience began to scream and rush to exit the building. The fire "alarm" was a prank. In the crush of people running for the exits, seven people were trampled to death and 28 others were severely injured.[44]

This horrific event weighed heavily on Spurgeon. He was tormented by nightmares and spent hours weeping in sorrow for quite some time. While he did return to preaching just two weeks after the tragedy, Spurgeon bore the emotional scars of this disaster for the rest of this life. He wrote later that for a good deal of time afterward, even the sight of the Bible made him cry.

While the Surrey Hall disaster certainly contributed, Charles suffered severe bouts of depression throughout his life. Today, he would have likely been diagnosed with clinical depression. When describing his depression, Spurgeon said, "I do not suppose there is any person in this assembly who ever has stronger fits of depression of spirits than I have myself personally."[45] He also suffered with gout, rheumatism, and Bright's disease, which is similar to Lupus.

#8: Learn from the Lord's discipline

Instead of wallowing in misery, Charles Spurgeon looked for purpose in his pain. As the quote at the beginning of this chapter shows, he learned to consider his depression and illness a blessing. His suffering and pain allowed him to be sympathetic to others and be able to comfort them in their affliction. He even said, "I would venture to say that the greatest blessing that God can give to any of us is health, with the exception of sickness. Sickness has frequently been of more use to the saints of God than health has."[46]

The longer you live, the more scars, both emotional and physical, you earn. Because we live in a fallen world, pain, sickness, and death are inevitable. No one is immune. Jesus did not promise a life of ease. On the contrary, He promised a life of trouble. This is often difficult to hear and even more difficult to experience. We would prefer to put our lives on cruise control and serve the Lord without any potholes, curves, or detours along the way. Martin Luther helped put this in perspective when he said, "They gave our Master a crown of thorns. Why do we hope for a crown of roses?"[47]

Jesus clearly told us what to expect. He emphatically said, "In the world, you will have trouble". Now, the good news is that He did not end His sermon with that thought. In His very next breath, He said, "But take heart! I have overcome the world."[48] The key for Christians, is not whether or not they will leave this life with scars, but how they handle the pain and suffering they are guaranteed to experience.

When we are faced with tragedy, illness, or other pain, we can retreat into ourselves, mope, and become bitter. Or we can go to the One who has overcome the world. We can cling to the Solid Rock and get through it, knowing we will eventually be made whole on the other side. Oswald Chambers explained our options eloquently when he wrote:

> *We all know people who have been made much meaner and more irritable and more intolerable to live with by suffering: it is not right to say that all suffering perfects. It only perfects one type of*

#8: Learn from the Lord's discipline

person – the one who accepts the call of God in Christ Jesus.[49]

Has your suffering perfected you? Not if you are still human. But you are probably better because of it. Don't be discouraged if you feel your testing, trials, and pain haven't yet made you perfect. Remember, even the Apostle Paul knew he was not yet perfected. However, as Spurgeon discovered, one of the best ways to heal and find purpose in your wounds is to use your pain and brokenness to sympathize with and comfort others. Paul clearly understood the purpose in his pain when he said:

Praise be to the God and Father of our Lord Jesus Christ, the Father of compassion and the God of all comfort, who comforts us in all our troubles, so that we can comfort those in any trouble with the comfort we ourselves receive from God[50].

You may be bleeding, metaphorically, or you may be scarred physically. Scars indicate a healed wound. Time can heal, if you let it. Think of some of the emotional and physical scars you bear. These scars are there to remind you of the painful events that caused them. If some of your scars are your fault, they can be a great reminder of how much wiser you have become. Fortunately, the farther in the past the wound occurred, the more it should be healed and the less painful it should be. Sometimes, if it were not for the scar, recalling the painful event may even be difficult.

Realize that God can use your scars to help others, just as Paul suggested. Who better to comfort someone who is going through a devastating divorce than someone who has gone through the same thing? Who better to comfort someone who has lost a child, parent, or spouse than someone who has also lost a child, parent, or spouse? Having gone through the same or similar pain gives you to ability to feel what that individual feels because you know firsthand what they are going through. Experiencing the same thing also gives you credibility in their eyes, because you successfully navigated those treacherous waters. You survived without drowning in your sorrow. You're not just giving them platitudes, you are giving them advice gained from your own experiences.

#8: Learn from the Lord's discipline

If you have ever watched a nature show about lions or elephant seals, you have probably seen images of the alpha males in the pride or pod. Often, they exhibit many scars, some of which are almost disfiguring. These scars are the result of many successful battles to maintain their status. The older these individuals, the more scars they display.

The same is true of us. The older we are, the more life experiences we've had, then the more lessons we've learned on our way to becoming wiser. And, since life and the lessons we learn are sometimes painful, more life experiences mean more scars and brokenness. If you are scarred from head to toe, rejoice. You have many ways you can serve the Lord by being a comfort to those injured in the same way.

Until shortly after my 46th birthday, I bore very few scars, either physically or emotionally. There were some serious struggles during the first three years of my marriage that left some very large, mostly self-inflicted, scars, but after that my life was relatively pain free.

However, my blessed life was not necessarily a blessing. During that time, I taught Bible classes for adults, led Bible studies in my home, discipled new believers, and served on several committees and boards at my church. Soon though, I began to develop the attitudes of pride and arrogance I have already mentioned.

My pride and arrogance manifested itself in three main areas; Bible knowledge, raising children, and handling finances. When it came to Bible knowledge, I began to develop a feeling of superiority, thinking I knew more about the Bible than most members of the church. I often left Sunday services with a critical heart, feeling the pastor had misspoke or was completely incorrect on some point. I was also beginning to look down on the other church members because they did not know as much as I did. How could they call themselves Christians when they barely knew anything? I had little tolerance of those who did not possess an in-depth knowledge of the Word, as I thought I did.

#8: Learn from the Lord's discipline

When it came to raising children, I knew I was the best parent ever. My children were the best behaved and, because I was training them up correctly, I was sure they would always follow the Lord. I was doing my part superbly. I had no compassion or sympathy for some of the older people in church who always seemed to be asking prayer for their prodigal children. I was convinced that if they had simply raised them right to begin with, they would have no need to be worrying about their children's spiritual condition now.

When it came to money, I had no sympathy for those who asked for prayer about their finances. I could not understand why they just did not get another job instead of complaining about being unemployed, or barely making it at their current job. If the individuals asking for prayer were self-employed, I was convinced they should just work harder. Maybe they should attend college at night, like I had, and get started on the path to a better paying career.

Sharing my sins of pride and arrogance is not easy. I am baring my soul to keep me humble and to show how God taught me very important lessons and broke me through these failings. Many of the scars and brokenness I now live with show me that the Lord did not give up on me. He was not content to have me wandering a road that did not lead to spiritual maturity, let alone perfection.

As we've already discussed, becoming more like Christ requires discipline. And when I did not have the self-discipline I needed, God provided His own discipline. While I did not necessarily think so at the time, I now understand His discipline showed His love for me. It showed that He accepted me as His son and wanted the best for me. It also shows He is committed to complete what He started in me.[51]

When it comes to spiritual growth, I am one of those individuals who, using my wife's terminology, learns by correction. As I think over the lessons the Lord taught me over the last few years, I recall Jesus saying, "Do not judge, or you too will be judged. For in the same way you judge others, you will be judged, and with the measure you use, it will be measured to you."[52]

#8: Learn from the Lord's discipline

I understand what Jesus meant in this passage much better now than I did 15 years ago. In my arrogance I judged others in these three areas; Bible knowledge, raising children, and finances. It was in those same areas that many of my painful lessons occurred. Some of my pain and brokenness was the result of living in a fallen world, and I can take comfort in knowing I did not cause everything that occurred, but these also helped me learn to turn to the Lord and put my faith in the Rock.

In the winter of 2005, my son was attending a Christian college in the South. My daughter had one more year in high school. My then wife, also a late bloomer, had completed a master's degree in history three years earlier and was teaching part-time for a local university. Life was good, until it was not.

It began with a phone call on a Saturday morning. My wife's only full sibling had taken his own life. He had struggled substantially with depression. He was often the recipient of my critical judgments as I lambasted him for making bad decisions. The guilt my wife and I felt after this was gut-wrenching. The "if onlys" and "what ifs" were with us for months. Tears came unexpectedly. My wife, for good reason, took this much harder than I did. My hard heart was ever so slowly beginning to soften. I was beginning to learn some painful lessons. I was beginning my time of the Lord's discipline.

Three months later, my wife's younger half-sister, whom she grew up with and cared for, was diagnosed with leukemia. Her prognosis was uncertain due to other health complications already faced.

Five months after her sister's diagnosis, my wife was diagnosed with a very fast-moving, rare, and essentially incurable variety of lymphoma.

My hard heart became a little softer. Those seemingly endless prayer requests for ill loved ones I had often previously critiqued at church took on much more meaning. Most of my prayers were for my wife and her sister, but I now offered occasional prayers for other people suffering illness, especially cancer.

Between the diagnosis of my wife and her sister, my son returned home from his first year at the

#8: Learn from the Lord's discipline

Christian college saying that his religion classes there had helped shatter his already struggling faith. He no longer professed to be a Christian and no longer had any desire to attend church. I, just like so many others whom I judged for bad parenting, was now praying for a prodigal child.

Over the next several months, my wife was in and out of the hospital either for treatments or to deal with her body's adverse reaction to those treatments. After only three of the scheduled five rounds of treatment, her doctor suggested it was time to quit. Any more and the chemotherapy would have done what the cancer was trying to do, kill her. Ten months after her cancer diagnosis, at the age of 47, and after 28 years of marriage, my wife passed away. When the end came I was absolutely devastated, even though I had started the grieving process months earlier. Yet I held onto the hope that she was with the Lord and that I would see her again. This fact helped ground me, but it didn't lessen the pain of her loss.

Six months after my wife passed away, her sister lost her battle with leukemia. She professed faith in

Christ during her illness and that provided spiritual comfort, though it did little to lessen the shock of the two previous years.

As widowers often do, I remarried quickly, just eight months after my first wife's passing. Tracy was also widowed about a year and a half before we married. She also lost a younger brother to a surprise heart attack the same day my sister-in-law passed.

When Tracy and I married, neither of us were far away enough from our loss to have scars. We both had very fresh wounds. Our relationship began at a distance with each of us comforting the other for a few months via email and phone calls before we met in person. After we married, sometimes our sadness and grief were just below the surface. At other times, the sorrow broke though and resulted in times of mutual sobbing.

These events left me broken and scarring. In my pain, I noticed my heart was softening to others. I thought I had learned everything God wanted me to. I prayed this would be all the discipline needed. But the

#8: Learn from the Lord's discipline

Lord had one more lesson in store for me, one more area of my pride and arrogance to deal with.

Over the next two years, I poured myself into my business. I expanded it, hired several employees, and increased it to over $1 million in revenues. At the beginning of the Great Recession of 2008-2009, my business grew rapidly. I enjoyed the fruits of my labor. I purchased a motorcycle, traveled, and moved to a larger house.

As I watched other industries and businesses retract and close during these difficult years, I thought we would be immune to the tumult. I listened unsympathetically to the personal stories of financial ruin as the economy slowed. I smugly thought to myself, they should have had the foresight to start a business in my industry. Had I spent more time in the Old Testament, I would have seen this warning, *"The Lord Almighty has a day in store for all the proud and lofty, for all that is exalted (and they will be humbled)."*[53]

Three years into my new marriage, my business began to collapse. Soon it was providing me with no income at all. Bills began to go unpaid. My entire retirement plan had consisted of real estate and my business. The home we recently purchased and the rental properties I had were now worth less than what I owed on them. All the net worth I previously had suddenly evaporated.

Deciding I should get a job to provide income, I applied and interviewed several places but was not hired. By the time this lesson was over, we had lost everything, our home, rental property, vehicles, and anything else of value.

Everything I had been arrogant and prideful about, and then some, were stripped away from me. This was a very difficult five-year period. It took another two years and almost two dozen interviews before I was finally hired into a full-time position. Taking that position required moving to a small town, three hundred miles away from family. I moved into this town and started a new job. I arrived in this new town broken, scarred, and far less arrogant and prideful than I was a few years earlier.

#8: Learn from the Lord's discipline

Almost a year after moving and starting my new position, we began attending our current church. Prior to this time, I was still healing and had not been involved in ministry of any kind. While my faith remained strong, I felt quite numb during these years. I did not feel I had anything beneficial to share with others because I was still healing myself.

Deciding it was time to once again become active in serving the Lord, I attended an evening men's Bible study. At the very first meeting, we broke into small groups and began to share. One of the men in my group revealed he had been laid off a few months earlier and was really struggling financially. Another asked prayer for his son who was not serving the Lord. A third man shared that he had been widowed a few years earlier. He also requested prayer for a prodigal son. As I listened to the real concerns and hurts, I knew I had changed. My pain and the discipline I received from the Lord allowed me to feel genuine sympathy for these men instead of judging them harshly, as I would have in the past. I came through that time of discipline with a changed heart. No, I haven't yet arrived, but I am making progress, pressing on toward the goal.

My new attitude of humility and brokenness, along with my willingness to be used of God in this new place, opened areas of ministry I would have never imagined. Before I knew what was happening, I was leading a home group, meeting with men one-on-one, teaching adult Sunday school classes, and starting a Bible School. Incidentally, the members of our home group have all been severely broken. We have individuals who are widowed, recently divorced, struggling with dying and prodigal children, as well as all the normal issues we face in a broken world. My heart is much softer than it was several years ago. I am able to listen, sympathize, and comfort because I too have gone through some of these painful issues and I have the scars to prove it.

My story is not unique. You may have suffered far more and bear deeper and more substantial scars than I do. But my story illustrates that God does not leave us where we are. He wants to mold and perfect us. Even if that means chipping away portions of our

#8: Learn from the Lord's discipline

life and maybe even breaking us to make us more like Him.

Sometimes it takes time to heal before we are ready to jump back into ministry and be used of God. This is normal, and I am sure God understands. For me, it took almost six years before I was ready to step out into service again. Other people can be used of God even while they are going through the deepest part of their pain.

I mentioned my friend Rick in a previous chapter. His wife's son, whom Rick considers his own, was diagnosed with brain cancer six years ago. The doctors gave him a year to live. He beat those odds. A few months ago, he had a checkup that showed the tumors in his brain had returned and were growing rapidly. Rick and his wife are now facing the very real possibility that their son will pass away soon. Rick and his wife are in the midst of their pain. This wound has not yet even developed a scab.

As Rick deals with the harsh reality of his son's eventual passing, others in his sphere of influence are noticing how he is dealing with it. The group of bikers

Rick rides with have noticed. In fact, he has been asked several times how he can hold it together when he knows his son will soon be gone. Rick's answer is very simple, "I am very sad, but my son loves the Lord and I know he will be in heaven when he passes. I'll get to see him again there too." It is no wonder Rick was asked to serve as the group's chaplain.

Think about the pain you have experienced and are experiencing. Think how you can use it to comfort others as you have been comforted by the Lord and others. As an older individual with many scars, you have multiple ways you can sympathize with and comfort others who need comforting. While we may not be able to see the complete picture here on earth, we can take comfort in the fact that "in all things God works for the good of those who love him, who have been called according to His purpose."[54]

Clay Jones in discussing Romans eight in his book "Why Does God Allow Evil", makes this interesting observation:

Paul answers that our enduring hardship and suffering, far from being evidence that God

#8: Learn from the Lord's discipline

> *doesn't love us, is exactly a sign of His love because we conquer through them. In fact, Paul has said it has been "granted" to us to suffer for Christ. In other words, our suffering is God doing us a favor.*[55]

You may not be ready to consider your pain a gift from God, but this is a very interesting way to look at it. If we begin to look at our wounds as gifts from God, as Charles Spurgeon did, we will heal faster. We can then use our past pain to encourage those who need encouragement. You have a wealth of experience and are living proof that God will help His children endure. Learn the lessons God has intended to teach you and help others avoid the same lessons if possible. Your past is valuable. Share it as you comfort others going through similar difficulties.

#9

Don't fear the future

Have I not commanded you?
Be strong and courageous.
Do not be afraid; do not be discouraged,
for the Lord your God will be with you
wherever you go.
Joshua 1:9

#9: Don't fear the future

What does the future have in store? The only truly honest answer to this question is we don't know. You may have plans and even preparations in place, but by now you have lived long enough to know that life doesn't always follow the plan you laid out. Your future is unknown and uncertain. Illness, an accident, lightning, or any number of other things can strike quickly and unexpectedly. The life and future you had planned can change in an instant. As believers, we know our future is in God's hands and that He has our best in store, but still, we can sometimes fear the unknown.

Fear is normal, even healthy at times. Walking through the Idaho desert or forest, I have a reasonable and healthy fear of treading on a rattlesnake. When I take my forty-seven-year-old boat out fishing, I have a healthy and reasonable fear my main engine may die of old age before I get back to the dock. When I am on my motorcycle, I fear another deer may decide to jump out in front of me. Yet even though these activities elicit fears, I still engage in them.

Some fear motivates us into action and that can be a good thing. I wear a helmet when I ride. I have a small spare motor on my boat. I watch where I walk. I pray for my unsaved loved ones, friends, and coworkers.

Improperly dealt with, fear can lead to inaction. It can keep us from stepping out of our comfort zone. If we don't control fear, it can control us. It can keep us from becoming effective workers in the Kingdom of Christ. Billy Graham once said, "Fear can paralyze us and keep us from believing God and stepping out in faith. The devil loves a fearful Christian."[56] By the way, Graham was 88 years old when this book was released.

I used to fear losing someone I loved dearly. I used to fear losing everything in a financial crisis and having to start completely over. Been there, done that. I survived. Was it painful? Of course. But now that I have made it through some very difficult times with God's help, I have noticed my fears are not as

#9: Don't fear the future

prevalent in my life as they once were and I am getting better at giving Him control of those things I can't control. Even so, I still try to retake control too often, and that leads to fear.

The aging process you are, or will be facing, is challenging. It is full of unknowns and potentially fear provoking. Alzheimer's? Heart attack? Cancer? Arthritis? You are probably beginning to understand that, unless Christ returns soon, you will leave this earth spiritually before you do so bodily. And the older you get, the closer that time approaches.

While you may not fear death because of the hope you have within you, you may fear the process of getting home to heaven. Take comfort though in knowing your future is in God's hands. Just as you have the hope of your resurrection and eternal life in heaven, you also need to have faith that God will see you through everything.

Look back at everything in your life the Lord has already brought you through. Remember how He uses your scars and pain to make you better. You will get through it. Take heart in knowing that He has promised to be with you in all things and to give you the strength to finish well.[57]

Sometimes fearing the future can make us retreat into and long for the past, even when that past was quite terrible. The Israelites, for example, after they were freed from their slavery in Egypt, faced an uncertain future. The only life they had ever known was that of being slaves. And as awful as their situation was in Egypt, whenever things got tough on their journey to the Promised Land, they pleaded to return. Even if that meant becoming slaves again!

Fear of the unknown caused the Israelites to long for the familiar. They had grown accustomed to life in Egypt. It was predictable. Even though life in Egypt was difficult and meant bondage, their fear made that old life seem more attractive than an uncertain future following Moses into an unknown land. Their fear kept them from trusting God, who was visibly with them and performed many miracles they witnessed for themselves.

When we fear the future, our true recollection of the past can fade. We replace the ugly truth with a

#9: Don't fear the future

glamorized, white-washed version of our past. We can see this happening with the Hebrews in the book of Exodus.

In the fourteenth chapter of Exodus, we read that Moses led the freed slaves to the edge of the Red Sea. It is interesting to note that in the previous chapter we see God specifically avoiding the shortest way to the Promised Land because that would require passing through hostile territory. He told Moses, "If they face war, they might change their minds and return to Egypt."[58] God was trying to prepare Moses for what he had in store in dealing with this fearful group of people.

Prior to arriving at the edge of the Red Sea, the Israelites had seen God release them from captivity in a miraculous way. Their firstborn sons were spared when all of Egypt's were killed. The Egyptians were so happy to see them leave, they gave them anything they requested. Since their exodus God had been leading them with His very presence -a cloud of smoke and a pillar of fire. God had been with them and continued to be with them.

Well done: Ten keys to remaining faithful to the end

God had led the people to the edge of the Red Sea where they were encamped. They were not sure what they will do next. They could not go forward. They have no boats and it was too far to swim. As they began to let fear of the unknown fill their hearts, they looked back toward Egypt. At least, they thought, they knew what to expect there.

As the people feared the way forward and were looking back at Egypt with fondness, they noticed Pharaoh's armies pursuing them. The sight of Pharaoh's army coming after them terrified them, even after all they have been through and had seen God's miraculous power. In their fear, they did do one thing correctly. They cried out to God.

We are not told what they said to God, but we do know what they said to Moses. Certain they were all about do die gruesome deaths at the hands of Pharaoh's army, they whined:

> *Was it because there were no graves in Egypt that you brought us to the desert to die? What have you done to us by bringing us out of Egypt? Didn't we say to you in Egypt, 'Leave us alone;*

#9: Don't fear the future

> *let us serve the Egyptians'? It would have been better for us to serve the Egyptians than to die in the desert!*[59]

In this passage, the Hebrews remember and acknowledge their status as slaves. However, because of their fear, they seem to prefer slavery to an uncertain future with Moses and God leading them. Fear and their lack of faith has paralyzed them. They are not interested at all in what God has in store for them in the future. In their fear, they are sure He brought them to the edge of the Red Sea because there was no room to bury them in Egypt. They are sure God is going to abandon them now. Fear clouded their thinking.

God, of course, heard their pleas and rescued them. They walked across the Red Sea on dry land. Once again, God showed them His power.

While they were still on the shores of the Red Sea trembling in fear, the Israelites remembered they were slaves when they were in Egypt. But they reasoned slavery would be better than being killed. Before long, though, it seems the bondage and hard labor they experienced in Egypt faded from their memories. They began to idealize their condition in Egypt, making it seem better than it was. It appears they even completely forgot they were ever slaves. After fear warped their memories of Egypt, they began to recall living a life of ease there.

We see this happening just two months after they crossed the Red Sea with that spectacular manifestation of God's power. This time, we read they complained about the food God miraculously provided every morning. It was not good enough. They grew tired of the same sweet-tasting manna. They wanted more variety, maybe a grand buffet. They grew to despise what God provided. Once again, they lodged their complaints to Moses:

> *If only we had died by the Lord's hand in Egypt! There we sat around pots of meat and ate all the food we wanted, but you have brought us out into this desert to starve this entire assembly to death.*[60]
>
> *If only we had meat to eat! We remember the fish we ate in Egypt at no cost—also the cucumbers,*

#9: Don't fear the future

> *melons, leeks, onions and garlic. But now we have lost our appetite; we never see anything but this manna!*[61]

By this time the Israelites had romanticized their time in Egypt. They remembered it now with great fondness. There is no mention of hard labor, slavery, making bricks without straw, or being beaten by harsh taskmasters. No, all they remember now was sitting around all day long gorging themselves on tasty morsels of meat, fish, melons, and anything else they desired to eat. And it was all free. It cost them nothing! The kind Egyptians cared for their every need.

We see something similar in the twentieth chapter of Numbers. In this passage the Hebrews were fearful they would run out of water. In issuing this complaint to Moses, they mentioned the grain, figs, and pomegranates they had in Egypt[62]. Hyperbole? Perhaps, but it shows exactly how fearing the future can lessen your effectiveness and stifle your use for God. Fear can create a longing for the past and keep you from pushing forward toward your future goal.

Well done: Ten keys to remaining faithful to the end

As we age, we shouldn't spend our lives looking back on the past, wishing things were as they were before. Yes, we can recollect with fondness, but we must look and move forward. Our best days can still be ahead. We must live this way every day, or we will become ineffective.

You've probably known people whose circle of interest shrinks as they age. They seem to become concerned with only the things going on immediately around them, which are often health related. These people often become fixated on the past when things were better. Their health was better. Life was simpler. These people seem to have no ability to move ahead. Their fear of the future keeps them from realizing the great things God may have in store for them in their last days.

As much as we miss the past, we can't go back. If fact, we shouldn't want to. If we are maturing daily and progressing toward our goal of knowing more of Christ and becoming more like Him, why would we want to return to our previous, less mature state?

#9: Don't fear the future

The Israelites complained constantly during their wilderness journey and longed for their distorted memory of Egypt. When they left Egypt, they crossed the Red Sea on dry land. The odds were pretty good they would not be returning to Egypt the same way. That road was closed. That door was shut. Returning to Egypt was impossible and surely they realized it. Yet, that didn't prevent them from dwelling on a false image of the past, which was preferable to moving ahead into the unknown. They let fear rule which kept them from believing the two faithful spies, Caleb and Joshua. It was their fear that cost them forty years in the wilderness.

Your past is the same. Doors have been shut. Roads are closed. Children grow up and make their own decisions, move away. Job losses, deaths, illnesses, and accidents are not going to unhappen. We can't move backwards. We can either move forward or remain stagnant. Of course, you know by now that God's desire is that you press on forward toward the goal of earning an eternal crown. This is very likely what Jesus meant when He said, "No one who puts a hand to the plow and looks back is fit for service in the kingdom of God."[63]

Even though facing an unknown future can be fearful, we need to keep our focus on the One who holds the future. We need to make the most of every opportunity until the day He calls us home. Billy Graham put it this way, "Old age has its challenges and is not for wimps, but God wants us to embrace it as part of His plan for our lives, and to look for the Lord's purpose in every circumstance and in every face or voice we encounter daily."[64]

Fearing the future can make us behave stupidly, or unwisely if you find stupid too strong a word. Fear can make us miss God's best for us. In addition to the Israelites wandering in the desert, the Bible gives us other examples of individuals who feared the future and lacked the faith to trust God fully. One of the best examples is the story of Ananias and Sapphira in the fifth chapter of Acts. As you might know, the story does not end well for these two. Their fear led them into stupidity and it cost them their lives.

#9: Don't fear the future

The first few chapters of Acts report the church began to grow rapidly after Pentecost. We are told that the believers in Jerusalem shared everything. Wealthier believers brought in money and gave it to the Apostles to provide for the common needs of the group. Those with land or houses sold their property and brought in the proceeds to the apostles to use as they saw fit for the betterment of the church and the expansion of the Kingdom. In doing so, the widows and orphans in the congregation received the care and provision they needed. No one in the church went hungry or was homeless. All of their basic needs were met through the generosity of those who shared their wealth.

Ananias sold some property. We assume, but are not told, this was the only property he had to sell. After receiving payment, Ananias and his wife Sapphira agreed to keep some of the proceeds. However, they decided not to tell the Apostles about the holdback. For some reason, they decided to claim they gave all they had received.

Well done: Ten keys to remaining faithful to the end

We can also only guess about the couple's motivation. Maybe they kept just a little aside for a rainy day, to send their son to Bible school, or for a vacation to the coast they had planned for next month. It was their anniversary after all.

More than likely Ananias and Sapphira were motivated to take this action because of fear. They were likely afraid to trust Christ with their future. What if this Christian thing fizzled out? What if hordes of poor people converted and placed a huge drain on the church coffers? There might not be any money for them when they needed it. They might starve or become homeless themselves. Not finding the idea of begging at the temple particularly attractive, they held some of the money back for themselves.

Ananias and Sapphira sinned, not because they held money back, but because they lied about it. They claimed that they gave all they received from the land sale. Their fear and lack of faith resulted in stupidity. Lying to God is a very serious offense and it could not go unpunished. Ananias and Sapphira became

#9: Don't fear the future

examples to the entire church of why you shouldn't lie to God. They also became the poster people of what happens when you let fear of the future rule your heart: you do stupid things.

When you are following God's direction for your life, your future, while unknown, can be exciting. As we have already discussed, you need to live your life realizing that your best days are yet to come. That does not mean you will be exempt from illness, pain, your eventual death and the deaths of your loved ones. It does mean that as you become more like Christ, the more He will use you. The larger your sphere of influence will become. The more you will be looked up to and sought out for your wisdom. The more you will be able to accomplish for the kingdom. *"Forget the former things; do not dwell on the past. See, I am doing a new thing! Now it springs up; do you not perceive it? I am making a way in the wilderness and streams in the wasteland."*[65]

#10

Pursue an eternal crown

If anyone builds on this foundation using gold, silver, costly stones, wood, hay or straw, their work will be shown for what it is, because the Day will bring it to light. It will be revealed with fire, and the fire will test the quality of each person's work. If what has been built survives, the builder will receive a reward.
I Corinthians 3:12 – 14

#10: Pursue an eternal crown

Aside from the Lord's direct intervention, your life's future path will be determined by the choices you make. For example, you can choose to retire from your career and the Lord's service when you hit that magic age. When that day comes you can enjoy life, take a much-deserved break, enjoy the fruits of your labor, and focus on yourself for a while. Or you can choose to continue pursuing the goal the Apostle Paul challenged all of us to strive for, an eternal crown, a heavenly reward, until there is no longer breath in your lungs or reason in your mind. You can choose to relax and take a break before you reach the finish line. Or you can commit to completing the race and to finishing it well.

Pursuing God's best involves making large, life changing decisions such as whether or not to retire from our job or our ministry. Ultimately though, pursuing God's best happens through the small choices we make daily. Every day we are faced with the choice to pursue the temporal or the eternal a gold watch or an eternal crown.

Well done: Ten keys to remaining faithful to the end

You face the decision to strive for the temporal or the eternal many times daily. Every minute of every day, you can choose what you will pursue; leisure, idleness, prayer, study, or something else. Certainly living with an eternal perspective is not easy. It takes effort. It means sacrificing comfort. It means you must constantly focus on and keep your eye on the finish line, the prize. Living with an eternal perspective simply means that "whatever you do, do it all for the glory of God."[66]

Billy Graham, in discussing aging, said this, "God doesn't want us to waste our latter years or spend them in superficial, meaningless pursuits. Instead, He wants us to use them in whatever ways we can to influence those who will come after us. He wants us to finish well, and one of the ways we do this is by passing on our values and our faith to those who will follow us."[67]

Pursuing the goal of knowing and serving Christ requires effort and discipline. It isn't easy. Paul compared it to a fight and an athletic competition. Fully pursuing Christ requires choosing how we spend

#10: Pursue an eternal crown

our time, energy, and finances daily. This is what it takes to allow us to come to the end of our journey and look back on a life well-lived for the Lord. We want to echo the words of Paul:

> *I have fought the good fight, I have finished the race, I have kept the faith. Now there is in store for me the crown of righteousness, which the Lord, the righteous Judge, will award to me on that day—and not only to me, but also to all who have longed for his appearing.* [68]

Paul, as we've already mentioned, used examples his readers could relate to, especially when discussing the Christian walk. He made it clear that whether it was boxing or running a race, only the finishers have a chance at receiving a victor's reward. Finishing well requires training, discipline, and keeping our focus on the prize. The prize Paul described and put all his efforts into achieving was an eternal crown. That too should be our goal. Not solely out of a sense of obligation, but out of love for the One who redeemed us with His own blood.

The Bible discusses crowns for believers in several places. In all, there are five heavenly crowns referenced in the New Testament. These are The Imperishable Crown[69], The Crown of Rejoicing[70], The Crown of Righteousness[71], The Crown of Glory[72], and the Crown of Life[73]. All these crowns are awarded in heaven and some appear to be earned through faithful and diligent service, as Paul suggests in his attempt to stir believers into action.

    So, does this mean that some people will have more rewards or crowns than others in heaven? This certainly seems to be the case. The passage from I Corinthians referenced at the beginning of this chapter, along with II Corinthians 5:10, seems to imply that our works for Christ will be judged and accordingly rewarded. Those who built their lives on eternal things; gold, silver, or precious stones will be rewarded. Those who built their lives on temporal things; wood, clay, hay, or straw, will receive no additional rewards. Please be sure to note that verse 15 in the third chapter of I Corinthians makes it clear that salvation is not what we are earning with our faithful service. Salvation is a free gift and cannot be earned.

#10: Pursue an eternal crown

Meditating on these passages, I can envision myself being rewarded for all my diligent work for the Lord. I am beginning to swell with pride, again. I imagine myself walking proudly around heaven with so many crowns I can barely keep them on my head. I have to stack my crowns, largest to smallest, and steady the pile with one hand as I stride past those with fewer or perhaps no crowns at all. I smirk just a little as I proudly walk by the crown impoverished. "How many times did you hear, 'Well done thou good and faithful servant'?" I ask as I smugly point to the stack of crowns teetering on my head.

That was a very bad attempt to elicit laughter. In reality, I will be one of the many who enter heaven smelling like smoke, "even though only as one escaping through the flames."[74] I take my eye off the prize far too often. I get entangled with worldly affairs. I waste inordinate amounts of time. I don't take advantage of every opportunity I am given to be an ambassador for Christ. I have numerous shortcomings. In an honest comparison between myself and the ideal set by Paul, I can only hold onto "Not that I have already obtained all this, or have already arrived at my goal, but I press on to take hold of that for which Christ Jesus took hold of me."[75] Thank God, He is faithful when I am not.

As we mature in Christ, we should want to please Him more and more. We realize that "we are God's handiwork, created in Christ Jesus to do good works, which God prepared in advance for us to do."[76] He delights in having His children build their lives upon and serve Him. And while He has promised eternal life to His followers, He has also promised to reward those who endure and finish well.

So will those who have earned heavenly crowns wear them with pride in heaven as I envisioned myself? Of course not. There is a passage in the book of Revelation that gives us some idea of what might really happen with our heavenly rewards. In Revelation chapter four, John records the following:

> *The twenty-four elders fall down before him who sits on the throne and worship him who lives for ever and ever. They lay their crowns before the throne and say:*
>
> *"You are worthy, our Lord and God,*

#10: Pursue an eternal crown

> *to receive glory and honor and power,*
> *for you created all things,*
> *and by your will they were created*
> *and have their being."*[77]

From this passage, it would appear that any heavenly rewards we obtain will be gratefully returned to Jesus, the only one worthy of receiving glory. Much like the parable of the bags of gold[78], it will be our pleasure to return to our Master what we have earned in His name. The emphasis, the gratitude, the glory, and the crowns will be His, not ours. Our motivation in striving for an eternal crown and heavenly rewards is not our own elevation. No, we are looking forward to, with profound and sincere gratitude, being able to present the rewards of a life well lived to the Lamb. The eternal crown we are pursuing is for His glory, not ours.

As I contemplated the amazing scene of vast multitudes in heaven laying their rewards at the feet of Jesus, I was reminded of an old hymn, "Crown Him with Many Crowns". I heard this hymn often as a child, but I can't recall the last time I heard it in church. The words of the first verse are:

Well done: Ten keys to remaining faithful to the end

> *Crown Him with many crowns,*
> *The Lamb upon His throne;*
> *Hark! How the heav'nly anthem drowns*
> *All music but its own!*
> *Awake, my soul, and sing*
> *Of Him who died for thee,*
> *And hail Him as thy matchless King*
> *Through all eternity.*

As I am reminiscing about old hymns I rarely hear anymore, one more came to mind. It is certainly a favorite of mine. The last verse and chorus of "The Old Rugged Cross" are:

> *To the old rugged cross I will ever be true*
> *Its shame and reproach gladly bear*
> *Then He'll call me someday to my home far away*
> *Where His glory forever I'll share*
>
> *So I'll cherish the old rugged cross*
> *Till my trophies at last I lay down*
> *I will cling to the old rugged cross*
> *And exchange it some day for a crown.*

#10: Pursue an eternal crown

Our mission is clear: Serve Christ until we are called home or unable to run the race any longer. When we retire from His service is up to Him, not us. He has work for us yet to do if we are willing to be used of Him. But being used of Him means we must remain unentangled, continue to sharpen our spiritual weapons, and realize He holds our future. Our lives should be a shining example of God's grace to those in our sphere of influence. Being faithful to the end, we can lay our crowns at the feet of the Lamb, fall on our faces and proclaim, "You are worthy, our Lord and God, to receive glory and honor and power forever! Amen."

I am coming soon. Hold on to what you have,
so that no one will take your crown.
Revelation 3:1

Learn more about the author or contact him at his website: www.LutherMaddy.com

[1] https://www.crosswalk.com/faith/spiritual-life/inspiring-quotes/20-powerful-quotes-from-charles-spurgeon.html
[2] Phil 3:10-14 (NIV)
[3] http://www.jewishencyclopedia.com/articles/3918-caleb
[4] Joshua 14: 6 – 12 (NIV)
[5] I Tim 6:17 (NIV)
[6] Matt 22:37 (NIV)
[7] Matt 22:39 (NIV)
[8] Mark 10:21 (NIV)
[9] Luke 14:26 (NIV)
[10] Matt 10:37-39 (NIV)
[11] Phil 3:8 (NIV)
[12] Matt 6:33 (NIV)
[13] Heb 11:39 (NIV)
[14] https://www.christiantoday.com/article/6-inspiring-christian-missionaries-who-gave-up-everything-for-christ/85936.htm
[15] https://thepastorsworkshop.com/sermon-quotes-on-the-bible/
[16] Studd, C.T. (1928), "The D.C.D"
[17] Acts 9:31 (NIV)
[18] II Cor 11:23–27
[19] Severance, Diane, Graves Dan, Dwight L. Moody was converted. Christianty.com https://www.christianity.com/church/church-history/timeline/1801-1900/dwight-l-moody-was-converted-11630499.html
[20] Deu 6:7 (NIV)
[21] Deu 6: 7–9 (NIV)
[22] Text from the Modeh Ani, a traditional Jewish prayer recited daily while still in bed.
[23] Deu 6:4 (NIV)
[24] Josh 14:11
[25] I Cor 9:24 - 27
[26] Carswell, Roger, Evangelical Times, "The life and legacy of Amy Carmichael, https://www.evangelical-times.org/40214/the-life-and-legacy-of-amy-carmichael/#event-j-h-newman

[27] Graves, Dan, Amy Carmichael, Kindly Kidnapper, Christianity.com. https://www.christianity.com/church/church-history/timeline/1901-2000/amy-carmichael-kindly-kidnapper-11630664.html
[28] Elliott, Elizabeth "A chance to Die: The Life and Legacy of Amy Carmichael", p. 49
[29] Bradfield, Haley, Amy Carmichael Biography. InspirationalChristians.org. https://www.inspirationalchristians.org/biography/amy-carmichael-biography/
[30] Carmichael, Amy, Gold by Moonlight, 1935
[31] Jerome, Commentary on Galatians 6:10
[32] II Kings 13:20
[33] McManus, Erwin Raphael, 2017, "The Last Arrow", Waterbrook, NY
[34] Proverbs 12:1
[35] Deu 32:35
[36] Numbers 11:11-15
[37] Proverbs 29:11
[38] James 1:5
[39] Proverbs 4:7-9
[40] https://en.wikipedia.org/wiki/Parkinson%27s_law
[41] Eph 5:15-16
[42] II Tim 2:4
[43] https://www.theopedia.com/charles-haddon-spurgeon
[44] https://www.christianity.com/church/church-history/timeline/1801-1900/spurgeons-service-at-surrey-gardens-11630503.html
[45] https://www.spurgeon.org/blog/posts/10-spurgeon-quotes-for-wounded-christians
[46] ibid
[47] https://www.christianquotes.info/images/martin-luther-quote-crown-of-thorns/
[48] John 16:33
[49] Oswald Chambers, Harry Verploegh (1990). "The Oswald Chambers Devotional Reader: 52 Weekly Themes", Oliver-Nelson Books
[50] II Cor 1:3-4
[51] Heb 12:6 & Phil 1:6
[52] Matt 7: 1-2
[53] Isa 2:12
[54] Rom 8:28
[55] Jones, Clay, 2017, "Why Does God allow Evil: Compelling Answers for Life's Toughest Questions", p. 197 Harvest House
[56] Graham, Billy, "The Journey: Living by Faith in an Uncertain World", Thomas Nelson, 2006
[57] Phil 4:13

[58] Exodus 13:17
[59] Exodus 14:11-12
[60] Exodus 16: 3
[61] Numbers 11:4-6
[62] Numbers 20:5
[63] Luke 9:62
[64] https://www.huffingtonpost.com/billy-graham/nearing-home-how-to-prepare-for-ones-latter-years_b_1031456.html1
[65] Isa 43:18-19
[66] I Cor 10:31
[67] https://www.huffingtonpost.com/billy-graham/nearing-home-how-to-prepare-for-ones-latter-years_b_1031456.html
[68] II Tim 4:7-8
[69] I Cor 9:24-25
[70] I Thes 2:19
[71] II Tim 4:8
[72] I Pet 5:4
[73] Jas 1:12
[74] I Cor 3:15
[75] Phil 3:12
[76] Eph 2:10
[77] Rev 4:10-11
[78] Matt 25:14-30

www.ingramcontent.com/pod-product-compliance
Lightning Source LLC
Chambersburg PA
CBHW051359290426
44108CB00015B/2073